Edition 5

By Hugh Kei

Disclaimer

Although the author has made every effort to ensure that the information in this book is correct at the time of publishing, the author does not assume and hereby disclaim any liability to any party for any loss, damage or disruption caused by errors or omissions, whether such errors or omissions result from negligence, accident or any other cause.

Copyright

Contents

About this TAM

This Tactical Aide Memoire has been written to help the Close Protection Officer produce a sound security plan and execute it successfully.

Tactics, techniques and procedures differ from operator to operator and team to team. Only you can decide what works best for your particular situation.

With that said, no two situations are ever the same and as such every plan should be revised and revisited at regular intervals. This TAM will help you ensure all aspects of security are addressed during the planning process.

You will notice throughout this TAM that key points and lists have Unique Numerical Identifiers (UNI's). The UNI's enable you and your team to quickly and accurately refer to general or specific information during all phases of the mission - aiding speed of communications and increased communication security.

3.1.12	Local A&E Department address	3.1.16	Local Police Point of Contact
3.1.13	Local A&E Department phone number	3.1.17	Local Police Department address / phone number
3.1.14	Will there be medical support on day of event?	3.1.18	Local embassy

Figure 1: CP TAM's Unique Numerical Identifier system (UNI)

The information contained within serves as a guide only: amendments and adjustments should be made where deemed necessary.

Acknowledgments

The author would like to thank the following individuals for contributing to this publication:

Charlie Curnow
Security and Investigations Professional
http://varsity-solutions.com

Wayne Scott Carr (Carzy)
Security and Investigations Professional
http://logasinternational.com

Aisling Foley
Trainee Solicitor at CMS Cameron McKenna

Nick McCarthy
Security Consultant
http://www.arguseurope.co.uk

Carl McGee
Security Consultant

Ryan Naish
Security Consultant
http://fitnesswins.net

Rachel Welford
Close Protection Officer

*For information on the author visit **hughkeir.com***

Section 1
Pre-Deployment

1.1
Personal Protection Officer Dress, Equipment, Alert States

Dress
- Dress for the occasion, it isn't always going to be a suit. If unsure, ask the Principal (better to ask than to be inappropriately dressed or worse - out dress the Principal)
- Ensure clothing fits correctly (ill-fitting clothes do not portray an image of professionalism and may hamper access to equipment on the person)
- High quality clothing will last longer, crease less and look better than cheap clothing. Buy cheap - buy twice.
- Clothing should have no emblems / logos or indication of nationality.
- Shoes should be treaded at all times. "Scoring" the bottoms of shoes does not work.

Hostile Environment Dress Considerations
- Full length trousers + long sleeved shirt (shirt may be required to fit over armour)
- Hard wearing, lightweight materials, preferably flash proof
- Flame resistant gloves
- High ankle lace up boots
- Ballistic protection sunglasses with changeable lenses (for night use)
- Rigger style tactical waist belt

Go-Bag + Equipment
A "go-bag" is packed at all times, on task or at home. It allows you to deploy at a moment's notice to the farthest reaches of the world knowing you have kit and equipment to last several days.
A go-bag should be a back pack / day sack - small enough to use as carry on baggage, large enough to hold the following list:
- Cash - Home currency and USD ($), you never know where you will end up, USD can be put to use almost anywhere, your home currency cannot (unless it happens to be USD).
- Credit card(s) with a good limit.
- Passport(s) (always try and keep one free of stamps or visas)

- Quad band dual-sim mobile phone (or a cheap mobile that will hold foreign sim cards)
- Solar powered charger with multiple adapters (for phone, laptop etc.)
- Travel plug
- Watch (capable of displaying different time zones without the need for manual adjustment)
- Compact first aid kit including: headache tablets, antiseptic cream, mosquito repellant, antihistamine, and sunblock.
- Purification tablets
- Compass
- Compact torch, good quality.
- Lighter
- Wash kit (ensure aerosols / liquids adhere to airport quantity restrictions)
- Sewing kit
- Lightweight blanket
- Note book and pen
- Laptop + Data Stick (8+ Gb)
- Camera
- Three pairs socks / underwear
- Spare shirt
- Boot polish
- Lightweight spray jacket
- Small umbrella
- GPS
- Spare batteries

Hostile Environment Equipment Considerations

- Slim line molle plate carrier and ballistic internal liner
- Minimum Level III Ballistic plates
- Single point sling (will attach to most assault rifles)
- Grab bags (minimal trauma kit, survival kit, emergency comms)

REMEMBER: Always pack your go-bag with the assumption you will be boarding a plane and will be subject to the standard security checks.

- All baggage should be plain civilian style items.
- Adorn all items of baggage with simple markers for quick identification at carousels. e.g. a strip of bright electrical tape placed around the handle (this includes the Principal's baggage).
- Nothing on your baggage should identify your nationality.
- Padlock all items.
- Keep all identification on your person, including copies.

- If possible obtain a second passport - Certain countries will not allows passengers entry if their passport contains certain other countries customs stamps. e.g. should you try and enter Israel with an Iranian stamp in your passport, your Principal will be conducting his trip without you! Always keep one passport for neutral countries if possible.

Alert States, Cooper's Colour Codes

The following alert states were penned by Jeff Cooper (former Marine Lt. Col.) and have been in use for a long time - for good reason. They are a simple, logical and effective way of describing maintaining the necessary level of awareness as a Protection Officer of any kind.

- White - 90% of "Joe public" are constantly in this state - oblivious to the environment and unprepared.

- Yellow   - The minimum alert state a Protection Officer should be in - a heightened state of situational awareness. No threat has been identified but you are constantly assessing the surroundings and potential threat development.

- Orange - You have identified a specific threat and now assessing possible developments, deciding on actions you may take to nullify or avoid it if required.

- Red - Responding to an attack, conducting an immediate action drill.

NOTES

1.2
Personal Protection Officer Responsibilities

- Gain and maintain the trust of the Principal.
- Brief the principal to a sufficient but not excessive level regarding security measures in place and "actions on". This may include rehearsals. Use KISS - Keep it simple, stupid.
- Provide a link between the Principal and the security detail.
- Liaise with the Team Leader / Operations Manager to ensure operational planning is conducted in a timely manner and is commensurate with the threat.
- Maintain morale and well being of the Personal Escort Section and through sound man-management ensure maximum performance is achieved at all times during operations.
- Ensure adequate protection of the Principal is maintained against all types of threat during your duty, including:
  - Physical (death, injury, kidnap)
  - Humiliation
  - Disruption
  - Destruction
  - Nuisance
  - Surveillance
  - Blackmail
  - Stalking
  - Intimidation (psychological)

REMEMBER
- Maintaining the trust of the Principal is paramount.
- A security-aware Principal will aid the smooth running of an operation.
- A paranoid or distrustful principal can significantly hinder an operation to the point of failure.

NOTES

1.3
Request for Information

This is a list of information you ideally wish to receive from the client upon acceptance of the mission or receipt of a notice to move.

Task Details

1.3.1	Type of Task	e.g. RST
1.3.2	Start Date + Time	If known
1.3.3	Notice to Move	
1.3.4	Task Duration	
1.3.5	Location of Task	If multiple, request likely start point
1.3.6	Future Intention	

Principal Specifics

1.3.7	Name	Of Principal
1.3.8	Physical Description	Age, Build, Clothing, Distinguishing features, Elevation, Face, Gait, Hair, Sex
1.3.9	Vehicle Description	Shape, Colour, Registration, Identifying Features, Make/Model
1.3.10	Medical Conditions	e.g. Angina, asthma, diabetes
1.3.11	Size of Party	Is the Principal travelling as part of a group - how many people?
1.3.12	Preferences	Likes / dislikes of the Principal
1.3.13	Routines	What patterns does the Principal set?

NOTES

Situation

1.3.14	**Known threats**	Threats already identified by Client / Principal
1.3.15	**Valuable items**	Items carried that affect threat assessment.
1.3.16	Laptop	Encrypted / backed up?
1.3.17	Smartphone 1	Password protected / backed up?
1.3.18	Smartphone 2	Password protected / backed up?
1.3.19	Briefcase	High quality, lockable or easily opened.
1.3.20	**Known to Joe Public?**	Is the Principal likely to be recognized in the street by the general public?
1.3.21	**Previous incidents**	What has led to the hiring of security?
1.3.22	**Circle of Knowledge**	Who else knows about the Principal's intentions i.e. who knows about the mission
1.3.23	**Pattern (through routine)**	Does the Principal's routine result in a predictable pattern of movement / behavior.

Logistical Requirements

1.3.24	**Number of vehicles in party**	If travelling as part of a group
1.3.25	**Types of vehicles**	4x4's / stretch, entry points: sliding doors / hatches etc. / berth?
1.3.26	**Drivers**	Names / skills. (If provided by Client)
1.3.27	**Source of vehicles**	Hire vehicles or Principal's own vehicles.
1.3.28	**Vehicle preference**	If PPO to source vehicles, does the Principal have a preference.

NOTES

Travel Details / Requirements

1.3.29	Special Requirements	Disabled seat, seat belt extension, vegetarian meal
1.3.30	Flight bookings / details	Do flights require booking or already done.
1.3.31	Other travel bookings details	Is the Principal planning on using any other mode of transport?
1.3.32	Principal Accommodation	Does accommodation need booking? Hotel preferences
1.3.33	Team Accommodation	Principal preference for accommodation location of security team
1.3.34	Luggage	Number of bags / miscellaneous items.

Point of Contact (POC)

1.3.35	Who to report to?	Should the PPO report to the Principal or a third party?
1.3.36	Frequency of reports?	How many and when?
1.3.37	Contact numbers	Of POC
1.3.38	Alternative numbers	Of POC
1.3.39	Email addresses	Of POC

Miscellaneous Info.

1.3.40	INTENTIONALLY BLANK	
1.3.41	INTENTIONALLY BLANK	

This information can now be used to begin formulating a Threat Assessment (Section 2.2).

NOTES

Section 2
Planning and Command, Control, Communications (C3)

2.1
Principal Profiling
(The 7 P's)

Much of the following information will not be immediately available but will be ascertained over time as the Principal's trust in you increases.

Personal History

2.1.1	Full name & title	2.1.9	Qualifications
2.1.2	Marital status	2.1.10	Positions held
2.1.3	Outstanding achievements	2.1.11	Previous spouse
2.1.4	Nationalities (previous/current)	2.1.12	Children (illegitimate?)
2.1.5	Languages	2.1.13	Medical history
2.1.6	Military service	2.1.14	Political history
2.1.7	Awards	2.1.15	Convictions
2.1.8	OTHER		

Personality

2.1.16	Provocative	2.1.22	Boastful
2.1.17	Mean	2.1.23	Arrogant
2.1.18	Dismissive	2.1.24	Violent
2.1.19	Ambitious	2.1.25	Fastidious
2.1.20	Devious	2.1.26	Vain
2.1.21	Brash	2.1.27	Methodical

People

2.1.28	Family	2.1.31	Friends	2.1.34	Loves
2.1.29	Rivals/Enemies	2.1.32	Business Associates	2.1.35	Social contacts
2.1.30	Employed staff	2.1.33	OTHER		

Places

2.1.36	Previous address	2.1.40	Birth Place	2.1.44	Home location

2.1.37	Education	2.1.41	Holiday destinations	2.1.45	Office location
2.1.38	Restaurants / eateries	2.1.42	Children's schools	2.1.46	Pubs / Bars / Clubs
2.1.39	Sports activities and destinations	2.1.43	OTHER		

Prejudices

2.1.47	Religion
2.1.48	Race
2.1.49	Culture
2.1.50	Controversial issues
2.1.51	Gender
2.1.52	OTHER

Private Lifestyles

2.1.53	Infidelities	2.1.56	Drinking habits
2.1.54	Gambling	2.1.57	Leisure activities
2.1.55	Workaholic?	2.1.58	Food & drink preferences
2.1.59	Narcotics	2.1.61	Sexual orientation
2.1.60	OTHER		

Political Views

2.1.62	Published opinions	2.1.66	Political ambitions
2.1.63	Open support	2.1.67	Memberships + Donations
2.1.64	Associations	2.1.68	Influence
2.1.65	Financial Investments	2.1.69	OTHER

NOTES

2.2
Threat Assessment

An accurate threat assessment is key if you are to produce an effective plan.

REMEMBER: as a Personal Protection Officer you are responsible for the complete well being of the Principal.

Do not overlook the everyday hazards they can be as dangerous for the Principal as a well-placed IED....

How safe is a Principal in his own home, with a 24/7 RST and support of the local authorities, if the relief PPO and newly hired chef are not aware of his extreme allergy to peanuts? Not very - even the smallest detail can be critical to the protection of the Principal.

A well-prepared threat assessment will ensure you have all the information required to produce a sound plan.

Aim of the Threat Assessment

- To identify the current and potential threats.
- Provide a foundation for operational planning.
- Identify operational requirements, including manpower, equipment and support.
- Identify prioritisation of tasking and resources.
- Identify current and potential vulnerabilities.
- Identify further information requirements and secondary Requests for Information (RFIs)
- Assess the probability of mission success.

General Points

- A definite assessment is not possible.
- To precisely determine vulnerability of the client and impact of an attack is difficult.
- Control and mitigate risk - completely eliminating risk is not possible.
- Threat assessments are an ongoing process.

NOTES

Principal Vulnerability Considerations

(Principal Profiling can be found in Section 2.1 and should be consulted along with these points)

2.2.1	Nationality / Race / Religion	2.2.7	Financial standing including debts
2.2.2	Home / Work locations	2.2.8	Lifestyle
2.2.3	Routes	2.2.9	Health incl. fitness, alcohol, stress
2.2.4	Vehicles	2.2.10	Associates
2.2.5	Legal Proceedings (past + present)	2.2.11	Infidelities / Indiscretions
2.2.6	Routines	2.2.12	Known adversaries

Other Considerations

2.2.13	Political Situation	2.2.17	Terrorism
2.2.14	Environmental Hazards	2.2.18	Principal's Business Activities
2.2.15	Standard of Current Security	2.2.19	Communications (phone / email / postal mail)
2.2.16	Crime Statistics	2.2.20	Family Feuds

Previous Incidents

2.2.21	Start of Incidents (Date)	2.2.26	Number of Incidents
2.2.22	Details of Incidents	2.2.27	Were incidents connected?
2.2.23	Target of incidents	2.2.28	Pattern of incidents (if any)
2.2.24	Action taken	2.2.29	Details of breach (if any)
2.2.25	Was there prior indication an incident was going to occur?	2.2.30	Did the incidents escalate in nature?

NOTES

Hostile Party Motivators

2.2.31	Politics	2.2.37	Religion
2.2.32	Culture	2.2.38	Crime
2.2.33	Jealousy	2.2.39	Obsession
2.2.34	Race	2.2.40	Provocation
2.2.35	Revenge	2.2.41	Grievance
2.2.36	Vendetta	2.2.42	Other

Threat identification

2.2.43	What	*What can happen*
2.2.44	How	*How can it happen*
2.2.45	Probability	*How likely is it to happen*
2.2.46	Impact	*How will it effect the operation*
2.2.47	Prevention	*How can you prevent it*
2.2.48	Nature of Threat	• *Specific / Non Specific* • *Imagined or Perceived* • *Paranoia* • *Circumstantial* • *Factual* • *Combination of the above*
2.2.49	Type of Threat	*Physical (death, injury, kidnap); Humiliation; Disruption; Destruction; Nuisance; Surveillance / Eavesdropping; Intimidation; Blackmail; Stalking; Intimidation (psychological)*
2.2.50	Who is at Risk	• *Principal alone* • *Family* • *Relatives* • *Associates*
2.2.51	What is at Risk	• *Business Interests* • *Home* • *Office* • *Property (including intellectual)* • *Reputation* • *Other*

NOTES

Categorize the Threat

Category 1
- Client is in significant danger
- An attack expected
- The impact of the attack would be serious or devastating

Category 1 protection recommendations:
- PPO
- Personal Escort Section (PES)
- Residence Security Team (RST)
- Security Advance Party (SAP)
- Office Security Team (OST)
- Armoured Vehicle
- Full Procedural, Technical and Physical cover

Category 2
- Is the client in some danger?
- An attack is possible
- Not 'when' but 'if'

Category 2 protection recommendations:
- PPO
- PES
- RST
- Category 1 measures as necessary

Note: Both CAT 1 and 2 involve 24/7 cover.

Category 3
- PPO
- PES and RST as necessary

N.b. This information serves as a guide: amendments and adjustments should be made if you feel it necessary. The checklists are not exhaustive and should be added to if the situation dictates. In addition, Categories 1, 2 and 3 can often be interlinked and are sometimes not clearly identifiable. This is the nature of threats and their assessment - rarely is a situation black and white. The information will however help you to conduct an accurate and effective threat assessment.

2.3
Planning Cycle and Miscellaneous Considerations

The Planning Cycle:

1.Notification of task
Receipt of task and dissemination of preliminary info. to team.

2.Threat assessment
Prepared from preliminary info and subsequently revised at regular intervals and at the presentation of new information. Identification of RFI requirements from client.

3.Initial liaison
With the Principal / Client or other representative. RFIs passed on at this stage if not already done so.

4.Reconnaissance and secondary liaisons
Recce's, additional third-party liaison if necessary and other information gathering / deconfliction tasks as required.

5.Warning order
Issued of Warning Order to team.

6.Operation order
Full orders to team.

7.Confirmatory recces
If required.

8.Final liaison
Confirmation of task, details and any changes to principal situation or unusual events.

9.Operation
Execution of the mission

10. Debrief and After Action Review (AAR)
Always conduct a debrief, including AAR for any incidents that may have occurred - minor or major. Allow team members to recite the mission from their point of view. This will prompt recollection of info. that may be useful for future missions.

AAR's are hugely beneficial for assessing

a) How an incident occurred,
b) How it could be prevented in the future
c) How it could be dealt with if an incident reoccurs.

Remember: every member of the team will have a different perspective on how a mission was executed. Everyone's experience is unique and different details are observed across the board. Use debriefs and AARs to gain as much information as possible and to instigate any amendments to the planning and execution to streamline your effectiveness as a team.

NOTES

Orders Structure

PRELIMS

Date of Mission
Map Folds
Weather
Team Composition (who is doing what)
Description of Area in General (overview to include brief outline of all routes and venues)
Description of Area in Detail (detailed relevant info)

SITUATION

Intelligence overview, recent incidents, previous incidents in the areas to be visited.
Threat update including enemy's Most Likely Course of Action (MLCOA), Most Dangerous Course of Action (MDCOA)
Atts / Dets: Police, Dogs, Search teams.

MISSION

Basic mission statement: "To protect .... in order to ...."
Multiple teams may require separate missions if not identical.

EXECUTION (Concept of Operations)

General outline: This will be a .... phase operation.
Name each Phase. e.g. Phase 1 - Preliminary moves, Phase 2 - Route Out
Phases in Detail: describe each phase in detail.
Summary of Execution: talk through the broad plan, reiterating key events or other details.

COORDINATING INSTRUCTIONS

Timings
Rehearsals
Equipment + Comms Check
Final admin points

NOTES

ACTIONS ON

Cover actions on for all phases. Talk through each action on phase by phase.
Don't overlook the basics: e.g. Mechanical failure, traffic accident.

SERVICE SUPPORT

Dress
Equipment
Weapons / Ammo
Vehicles
Maps
Personal kit
Accommodation
Feeding
Medical
Fuel
Luggage
Other points

COMMAND AND SIGNALS

Ops room location
Movement of Ops (if mobile)
Chain of Command
Comms frequency changes
Codewords
Nicknames
Nicknumbers
Synchronize watches

NOTES

2.4
Ops Room Equipment

A suggested list of Ops Room equipment: tailor to suit your requirements.

Communications

- Radio base station for each band in use
- Hand held transceivers (spares to supplement personal issue including chargers, batteries)
- Mobile Repeaters (if required)
- Comms ancillary equipment (e.g. earpieces, antennae, etc.)
- Satellite / Cell phones
- Landline telephone equipped with speed dial to Principal, Team leader, PPO and Local Authorities.
- Direct comms to Principal and safe room (e.g. intercom / direct landline).

Technical Equipment

- Powerful desktop computer and laptop + internet connection (laptop should be synchronized with PC)
- Security Monitors (only as many as necessary, one large screen may be sufficient)- both audio and visual dependent on technical security in place (e.g. CCTV, listening devices, intruder detection systems, personal alarm, room alarms etc.)
- Printer / scanner / fax combo
- Electronic Counter Measures (threat dependent)
- Mobile surveillance equipment (for rapid deployment)
- Building plans and schematics internal and external

Emergency

- First Aid Kit
- Fire fighting equipment
- Bomb blanket.
- Respirators
- Back up power system

Search Equipment

- Vehicle search eqpt.
- Baggage search eqpt.
- Room search eqpt.
- Passive Night Vision Equipment
- Torches

Documentation, Maps and Imagery

- Maps
- Air photography
- Mapping system, spots, traces, proven routes etc.
- Logs, records and reports including confidentiality agreements, details and photographs of all staff (e.g. daily occurrences, recce reports, surveys, incident reports, intelligence reports etc.)

NOTES

2.5
Communications

Communication Security

- Do not discuss operational details on unsecure means of communication (timings, Principals, teams strengths, vehicles, locations etc.)
- Use code names, never real names
- Codes must be unpredictable and random
- Change codes regularly
- Change channels frequently
- Check equipment daily
- Ensure the comms plan and equipment is suitable for the task (battery / mains power, band / frequency, secure / non-secure, covert / overt, all-informed net or separate channels etc.)
- Have a contingency plan for loss of primary comms that can be rapidly adopted.

Selecting a Frequency Range.

UHF - Suitable for short range built up areas (e.g. multistory building) due to limited broadcast range and reception. However, can reach vertically up to 30 floors dependent on structure and building material. Best operation with line-of-sight between users.

VHF - Little interference, suitable for short-mid range use (5 meters to a few kilometers dependent on signal strength and surroundings. Can function well without line of sight but often poor within buildings, dependent on structure and building material.

HF - Suitable for long ranges, does not require line of sight. Transmission range can be inter-continental, dependent on signal strength. Can be susceptible to significant interference. Performance also significantly affected by changes in the ionosphere, often most noticeable during transition from day to night and vice versa.

Radio Communications Licences

Some countries have strict licensing laws regarding radio communications, this includes the United Kingdom. Ensure you are aware of the legal requirements and the impact this may have on your communication security.

Mobile Phones

- If opting for a dual-SIM phone, ensure that a model is selected which allows simultaneous monitoring of both SIMs - "active dual-SIM", not "standby dual-SIM".
- If a smart phone is not required then don't buy one - battery life is generally much less than basic mobile phones.
- If a phone model is selected that contains a removable battery, consider purchasing a second battery as a backup.
- In addition, purchase in-car and USB chargers and a compact solar charger with multiple adapters, allowing you to charge your phone and other devices in locations without power.
- Network selection is key and depends upon your destination. Ensure you research before deployment.
- Unlocking your phone to function with multiple service providers will allow locally purchased SIM cards to be used, don't overlook this detail.
- Standard size SIM cards can be carefully trimmed down to the size of a micro SIM with a sharp blade, thus allowing their use in micro-SIM slots.

Voice Procedure(VP)

- The majority of comms you ill use will be insecure.
- If you are unsure of whether comms are secure or not then assume to be insecure.
- Keep natural pauses between sentences)
- Keep sentences short
- Don't speak to quickly
- Don't shout, it can cause distortion.
- Raise your pitch slightly.
- Think what you are going to say before you press transmit and **PRESS, PAUSE then SPEAK.**

Common Commercial VP

Alpha - Adult Male
Bravo - Vehicle
Charlie - Building / Structure
Echo - Adult Female
Foxtrot - On Foot
Mobile - Vehicle-borne
Plug - Child
Rucksack - Police
Scratcher - Dog

Common Military VP

- CALLSIGN - precedes a callsign name e.g. "Callsign E23"
- ACKNOWLEDGE - Requests acknowledgement of message from receiving callsign. e.g. "A1 static at Yellow 12, all callsigns acknowledge, over"
- CANCEL - Disregard e.g. "Cancel my last" = "Disregard my last message"
- CORRECT - "You are correct".
- RADIO CHECK - requests a radio check with specified callisign e.g. "E23 this is E22, radio check, over"
- GRID - precedes a grid reference e.g. "My location Grid 38R QU 22300 97199
- FIGURES - precedes digits e.g. "I will be at your location in figures one zero"
- I SPELL - Precedes letters when spelling a word that may be unclear over the net.
- SAY AGAIN - "Repeat your last message"
- CONTACT - Informs all callsigns you are engaged with the enemy
- DIFFICULT - "I can hear you but you are difficult to understand"
- UNWORKABLE - "I can hear you but not what you are saying"
- ROGER - "Yes/Ok/Understood
- OVER - "This is the end of my message, I require a reply from you"
- WAIT OUT - "I heard you, now wait for a response as I cannot immediately give one"
- OUT - I am ending the transmission and require no reply to this message."

NOTES

Section 3
Surveys and the Security Advance Party

3.1
General Survey Information Requirements

Basic Details

3.1.1	Name of Person conducting Survey	3.1.7	Date of Survey
3.1.2	Venue Name	3.1.8	Venue Website
3.1.3	Venue Address	3.1.9	Venue Phone number
3.1.4	Venue Point of Contact	3.1.10	Security Point of Contact
3.1.5	Arrival date / time of Principal	3.1.11	Departure date / time of Principal
3.1.6	OTHER		

Local Law Enforcement and Services

3.1.12	Local A&E Department address	3.1.16	Local Police Point of Contact
3.1.13	Local A&E Department phone number	3.1.17	Local Police Department address / phone number
3.1.14	Will there be medical support on day of event?	3.1.18	Local embassy
3.1.15	Emergency Service Response times	3.1.19	OTHER

NOTES

Arrival

3.1.20	Host / Principal Meeting Point (e.g. main entrance)	3.1.26	Will there be a receiving line / greeting ceremony?
3.1.21	Who will greet the Principal?	3.1.27	Will principal be allowed to bypass security, will baggage be searched?
3.1.22	Routes in / out for motorcade	3.1.28	Embus / Debus points
3.1.23	Parking area for motorcade	3.1.29	Press present during event?
3.1.24	Will Press be screened for credentials prior to entry?	3.1.30	Type of Press (stills/video/both/live or recorded)
3.1.25	Location of Press	3.1.31	OTHER

Infrastructure

3.1.32	Number of elevators (are there VIP elevators?)	3.1.42	Number of flights (of stairs) to floor
3.1.33	Elevator capacity	3.1.43	Number of stairwells
3.1.34	Will elevators be functioning during event?	3.1.44	Toilet locations
3.1.35	Exterior perimeter in place?	3.1.45	Is perimeter wall/fence/water feature/other?
3.1.36	Is perimeter continuous or are there gaps?	3.1.46	Height / width of perimeter?
3.1.37	Are any rapid deployment obstacles used at entry / exit points? e.g. caltrops,	3.1.47	Is the venue overlooked by other structures?
3.1.38	Is there dead ground to the security staff?	3.1.48	Are there parking areas in close proximity to venue?
3.1.39	Are parking areas in close proximity to perimeter or entry / exit points?	3.1.49	Does the venue use an airlock style entry / exit system?
3.1.40	Are all visitors / vehicles details recorded?	3.1.50	Are all visitors / vehicles searched prior to accessing the venue?
3.1.41	OTHER		

Alarm Systems

3.1.51	Is there a fire alarm system?	3.1.62	Is the fire alarm system monitored on-site or off-site?
3.1.52	Is the fire alarm system regularly tested?	3.1.63	When was the last test?
3.1.53	What types of detector are in use? (Smoke, heat, etc.)	3.1.64	Is it a zoned system?
3.1.54	Is there a fire suppression system fitted?	3.1.65	What type of suppression system is it?
3.1.55	What types of handheld fire extinguisher are in place and where are they?	3.1.66	Are the handheld fire extinguishers in place regularly inspected?
3.1.56	Is there an intrusion alarm system?	3.1.67	Is the intrusion alarm system monitored on-site or off-site?
3.1.57	What areas of the interior and external perimeters are not alarmed?	3.1.68	Is there a Public Address(PA) system that can be utilized in an emergency?
3.1.58	Who controls the PA system and where?	3.1.69	Is there a Closed Circuit Television System in place?
3.1.59	Is it a hard-wired or wireless system?	3.1.70	Is the system monitored 24/7?
3.1.60	What is the CCTV system used for?	3.1.71	Where is the CCTV system controlled?
3.1.61	OTHER		

NOTES

Venue Security Staff

(This information may not always be available but should be sought where possible)

3.1.72	Security Manager background?	3.1.82	Frequency of Security Manager / Supervisor meetings?
3.1.73	Frequency of Security Manager / Local Law Enforcement meetings?	3.1.83	Security staff provided by venue or private company?
3.1.74	Security staff licensing requirements?	3.1.84	Security staff training / qualification requirements?
3.1.75	Last training conducted when?	3.1.85	Last drill conducted when?
3.1.76	Are staff checked for criminal records?	3.1.86	Are security staff vetted for conflicts of interest etc.?
3.1.77	What is the leave duration?	3.1.87	What is the shift / rotation length?
3.1.78	Are the security staff uniformed?	3.1.88	Are security staff armed?
3.1.79	When / what was the last incident warranting a security response?	3.1.89	Do security staff carry identification?
3.1.80	What is the primary means of communication for security staff to supervisor and manager?	3.1.90	Are vehicles used by security staff? Markings / identification?
3.1.81	Are security staff trained in search techniques?	3.1.91	OTHER

Attach floor Plan / schematic if possible including:

• Security systems + infrastructure (lighting, perimeter defences etc.)
• Lines of communication and comms infrastructure (antennae, dishes etc.)
• Heating system
• Fuel / water inlets / outlets including storage tanks
• Access points including windows, garages, and door orientation
• Elevator locations

Now refer to the following site-specific sub-sections (3.2-3.6) where applicable.

3.2
Hotel Survey
Information Requirements

REMEMBER: The Concierge is a PPO's best friend during hotel stays - the resident 'fixer', there isn't much he can't achieve (if he considers it worth the effort). Work on this relationship from the outset.

Basic Details

3.2.1	General Manager Name / phone	3.2.4	General Manager email
3.2.2	Security Manager Name / phone	3.2.5	Security Manager email
3.2.3	Fire alarm/sprinkler system Y/N?	3.2.6	Control room location

Room details

3.2.7	Internet access / speed	3.2.12	Plug socket type and voltage
3.2.8	Acceptable payment methods	3.2.13	Public or Private venue (hotel / private apartment)
3.2.9	Room rate (Suite)	3.2.14	Room Rate (Single)
3.2.10	Laundry Rate	3.2.15	International call charges
3.2.11	Is breakfast included	3.2.16	What are the concierge services?

Other Services

3.2.17	Bell boys / porters?	3.2.22	Dry Cleaning?
3.2.18	Currency Exchange?	3.2.23	Gym?
3.2.19	Spa?	3.2.24	Pool?
3.2.20	Restaurant?	3.2.25	Room service?
3.2.21	Early check-in / late checkout?	3.2.26	Conference rooms?

NOTES

Miscellaneous Details

3.2.27	Will hotel relocate / exchange furniture as required by security?	3.2.35	Description of route from hotel entrance to Principal's room
3.2.28	Is there a separate area for baggage vehicles to load / unload	3.2.36	Is there a separate elevator for baggage
3.2.29	How will hotel security augment Principal's security	3.2.37	How will local authorities augment Principal's security
3.2.30	Details of guests staying adjacent and above/below Principal's room	3.2.38	Details of employees providing service to principal and staff
3.2.31	Location of room keys	3.2.39	Availability of room keys (time / date)
3.2.32	Where is a suitable Ops Room location?	3.2.40	Are there comms black spots?
3.2.33	Is the PPO's room situated appropriately in relation to Principal?	OTHER	

NOTES

3.3
Airport Survey
Information Requirements

Basic Details

3.3.0	Private or Commercial flight	3.3.3	VIP lounge Contact
3.3.1	Flights Ops Point of Contact	3.3.4	Airside Access Hours
3.3.2	Airport Hours of Operation	3.3.5	OTHER

Arrivals

3.3.6	Principal Arrival Time	3.3.14	Airline and Flight Number
3.3.7	Type of Aircraft	3.3.15	Terminal / Gate number
3.3.8	Tail Fin Number	3.3.16	Callsign
3.3.9	Staircase required for aircraft?	3.3.17	Staircase Point of Contact
3.3.10	Unloading procedure?	3.3.18	Is airport assistance provided (i.e. baggage handlers)
3.3.11	Luggage conveyor required?	3.3.19	Luggage Point of Contact
3.3.12	Will there be an arrival ceremony?	3.3.20	Who will attend the arrival ceremony?
3.3.13	Will there be an embassy representative to meet the Principal	3.3.21	OTHER

Customs

3.3.22	Customs Point of Contact	3.3.24	Customs procedure
3.3.23	Security Managers contact details	3.3.25	OTHER

NOTES

Departures

3.3.26	Principal's departure time	3.3.32	Will there be a departure ceremony?
3.3.27	Who will attend?	3.3.33	Staircase Point of Contact
3.3.28	Staircase required for aircraft?	3.3.34	Is airport assistance provided (i.e. baggage handlers)
3.3.29	Unloading procedure?	3.3.35	Will baggage be checked?
3.3.30	Where will baggage be checked?	3.3.36	How will baggage be checked?(X-ray, physical search etc.)
3.3.31	Can vehicles go airside for drop-off	3.3.37	OTHER

REMEMBER: Some security services in parts of the Middle East and Asia can offer much more assistance airside at airports than facilities elsewhere in the world. Liaise with key personnel at the earliest safe opportunity to make your Principal's transition a smooth one.

NOTES

3.4
Hospital Survey
Information Requirements

Basic Details

3.4.1	Hospital Name, address and telephone number	3.4.6	Religious affiliations
3.4.2	Ward telephone numbers	3.4.7	Security telephone numbers
3.4.3	Weapon policy?	3.4.8	Will PES be allowed to accompany the Principal at all times?
3.4.4	Payment details?	3.4.9	Is the hospital open for admittance 24/7?
3.4.5	OTHER		

Emergency Capabilities

3.4.10	Is there an emergency room?	3.4.20	Emergency room location?
3.4.11	General surgery specialist present 24/7?	3.4.21	Neurosurgery specialist present 24/7?
3.4.12	Emergency medicine specialist present 24/7?	3.4.22	Cardiology specialist present 24/7?
3.4.13	Radiology specialist present 24/7?	3.4.23	Thoracic surgery specialist present 24/7?
3.4.14	Orthopedic surgery specialist present 24/7?	3.4.24	Full trauma team present 24/7?

3.4.15	If no to any of the specialists - what are the response times?	3.4.25	Is the radiology department capable of completing a full diagnostic?
3.4.16	Number of acute injury treatment areas?	3.4.26	is there a CAT Scan?
3.4.17	Operating room location	3.4.27	Number of suites
3.4.18	Intensive care: surgical beds	3.4.28	VIP suite and location
3.4.19	OTHER		

Routine Treatment

3.4.29	Does the hospital routinely care for Major surgery	3.4.34	Does the hospital routinely care for Thoracic surgery
3.4.30	Does the hospital routinely care for Acute cardiac patients	3.4.35	Does the hospital routinely care for Severe burn patients
3.4.31	Does the hospital routinely care for Neurosurgery	3.4.36	Does the hospital routinely care for Severe trauma patients
3.4.32	If no to any of the above is there a transfer system?	3.4.37	To what hospital

3.4.33	When travelling internationally, special care should be taken about the source of the whole blood supply	3.4.38	OTHER

Access by air

3.4.39	Helo pad available	3.4.42	Helo pad location by address
3.4.40	Helo pad location by grid coordinates	3.4.43	Can helo pad be used 24/7
3.4.41	OTHER		

NOTES

3.5
Restaurant Survey
Information Requirements

Basic Details

3.5.1	Name of venue	3.5.13	Is reservation required?
3.5.2	Address + telephone number	3.5.14	Name of manager
3.5.3	Name of Maitre'd	3.5.15	Number / locations of public entrances
3.5.4	Number / locations of staff entrances	3.5.16	Location of restrooms
3.5.5	Location of telephones	3.5.17	Seating capacity
3.5.6	Seating arrangements	3.5.18	Menu and wine list
3.5.7	Dress code	3.5.19	Methods of payment (cash, credit card, check)
3.5.8	Private rooms	3.5.20	Smoking areas
3.5.9	Other events planned on same day visit	3.5.21	Name, address and telephone of nearest police department
3.5.10	Name, address, and telephone of nearest hospital	3.5.22	Where is the Principal's table, does it suit their preference
3.5.11	Where does the PPO need to be seated for line of sight to Principal	3.5.23	What is the emergency response time to the venue
3.5.12	OTHER		

NOTES

3.6
Maritime Survey
Information Requirements

Port Details

3.6.1	Port name + contact numbers	3.6.13	Port location, access roads and building floor plans
3.6.2	Dock open 24/7?	3.6.14	Documentation required?
3.6.3	Number of craft dock points	3.6.15	Names and registers of other port users (private/corporate/organisations)
3.6.4	VIP areas	3.6.16	Security services?
3.6.5	First aid point	3.6.17	Coast Guard alerts
3.6.6	Restrooms	3.6.18	Restaurants and shops
3.6.7	Foreign currency exchange stations	3.6.19	Car service locations
3.6.8	Size restrictions for craft	3.6.20	Overall condition of the port
3.6.9	Review past reports on prior trips	3.6.21	Operational hours
3.6.10	Waiting times for luggage	3.6.22	Waiting times for vehicles
3.6.11	Handling agent contact details	3.6.23	Harbor Master contact details
3.6.12	Customs contact details	3.6.13	Coast Guard policy

Vessel Details

3.6.24	Captain's name	3.6.28	Captain's contact details
3.6.25	Crew names	3.6.29	Have Captain and crew been vetted?
3.6.26	Vessel layout	3.6.30	Vessel facilities
3.6.27	Security systems	3.6.31	Travel schedule

3.7
SAP Composition And Search Equipment

Composition

- The size and composition of the SAP will be determined by the threat, the manpower available on the team and the size of the venue / location to be secured.
- Minimum of two men (Driver +1).

Hostile Environment SAP considerations

Dependent on the theatre of operations SAP teams will sometimes be local nationals. They will operate under command of the PPO and will often be equipped only with mobile telephone as the form of communication.

In such instances, strict operational security procedures should be applied when dealing with a local national SAP team, as vetting of these individuals is limited.

A local national's understanding of 'covert' isn't always the same as your own!

Search Equipment

These tools are essential to conduct thorough internal and external searches and where possible should be carried during all phases of the operation.

Security seals	Spanners	Pliers
Mallet + wedges	Screwdrivers incl. electric	Lock picks
Tweezers	Hacksaws	Tape Measure
Hammers	Socket sets	Drill + bits
Bolt croppers	Crow bars	Allen keys
Electrical tape	Gloves	Zip ties
Nails	Torches	String
Screws	Mirrors	Overalls

- You can also include technical search aids such as electronic surveillance detection equipment.

NOTES

3.8
SAP Procedure

Receipt of Mission

- SAP Commander to conduct a" face-to-face" meeting with the PPO or TL a.s.a.p.
- Carry out pre-deployment equipment checks, for example:
    Tracking systems
    Comms checks including crypto / frequencies
    Portable Intruder Detection systems
    Search equipment
- Request latest route recce report, threat assessment, intelligence reports if available.
- Confirm taskorg including Personal Security Detail and outside agencies.
- Confirm Principal's travel details including:
    Mode of transport
    Time of departure
    Transition times and locations,
    Intended route
    Alternative route.
    Up-to-date itinerary
- Confirm CEI and lost comms procedure including:
    Code words / nick numbers
    Contact details of venue / transport liaison
    Contact details of outside agencies
- Confirm identification / documentation requirements (checkpoints, borders, access lists)
- Dress Code

NOTES

Route Out

- Maintain comms with the PPO / PSD
- Note route discrepancies against route recce report.
- Reassess vulnerable points.
- Advise PPO as required

At Venue

- Inform PPO of SAP arrival at venue and establish control point / ops room if required
- Confirm embus / debus locations
- Liaise with venue staff if required including security and other agencies
- Check guest list
- Clear venue
- Confirm entry / exit points / cloakroom procedures
- Check escape routes
- Confirm alternative access between floors i.e. service elevators, emergency stairwells
- Confirm waiting /meeting / dining location if applicable
- Clear toilets and other locations to be used by Principal
- Identify / confirm safe room
- If venue plans / schematics are held, annotate as necessary to reflect changes / amendments. e.g. building extensions, removal of fire exit, relocation of car park
    Advise PPO as required.
  Note existing security procedures of the venue including: Fire, Bomb, Medical Emergency and location of First Aid equipment.
- If Press expected, identify out of bounds areas for Press as allocated by venue staff.
- Await arrival of Principal

Approach of Principal

- Confirm venue clear to PPO
- Civilian / traffic control as necessary

Arrival of Principal

- Guide PPO if required
- Adopt positions as directed by PPO or detailed in plan
- Await PPO instructions for next phase.

3.9
Searches

Technical Surveillance Counter Measure Search

If technical search aids are in use, never rely on them alone. Where time permits a full and thorough search should be conducted.

- Practice searching and establish a systematic approach to the task. Remember: above, below and 360 degrees.
- When examining electrical or mechanical items in the room, check to see if they are functional. Do they work properly? Non-function may indicate the item has altered in some way.
- Check every surface in the room visually and physically.
- Look for unnatural discoloration or changes in decorative patterns.
- For furniture such as sofas and even enclosed lamp shades you must get inside the item to search. Remove backing materials or partitions and visually check.
- Remove all drawers from closets and chests when examining.
- Check all electronic and communications cabling.
- Check inside the ceiling, check under the floor and false walls.
- Check functionality of alarm systems.

NOTES

Vehicle Search

1. Type, make, model, doors, year, body type
   - License number
   - Country
   - State
   - Location of security check
   - Date
   - Day
   - Search start time
   - Search end time
   - Searcher signature
2. Exterior scan of vehicle, hands off only
   - Signs of forced entry
   - Signs of tampering: fingerprints, scratches, and fluids on the ground, exposed or hanging wires
   - Area around and under each tire
   - Inspect telltale tape for breakage: doors, bonnet, and boot, wheel covers
3. Inspect vehicle undercarriage
   - Left front engine compartment and suspension
   - Right front engine compartment an suspension
   - Left rear engine compartment
   - Right rear engine compartment
   - Transmission
   - Drive shaft
   - Emission control system
   - Muffler, resonator, tailpipe
   - Differential
   - Rear axle and suspension
   - Wheels
   - Fuel tank
4. Search interior, physical check-rear seat
   - Doors
   - Door panels
   - Floor mats
   - Rear seat and armrests
   - Rear deck and speakers
   - Headliner
   - Headrests
   - Pillows
   - Dome light and dome light switches
   - Under front seat
   - Back of front seat

5. Search interior, physical check front seat
   - Doors
   - Door panels
   - Floor mats, pedals, and floor switches
   - Fuse box
   - Front seats
   - Dashboard areas, vents, ducts, and controls
   - Radio, radio speakers, lighter, and ashtrays
   - Glove compartment
   - Sun visor and headliner
   - Dome light and dome light switches
   - Headrests
6. Search boot area-physical check
   - Floor mats
   - Spare tire
   - Back of rear seats
   - Tool compartment
   - Electrical wiring
   - Underside of rear deck
7. Inspect fuel tank
   - Verify fuel cap in locked position and has not been tampered with.
   - Take off the cap and check the pipe.
8. Search engine compartment
   - Check at safety catch level
   - Check entire compartment

NOTES

Section 4
The Personal Escort Section

4.1
Personal Escort Section
Composition and Equipment

Composition

Composition of the Personal Escort Section will vary from task to task.

The PES is the outer cordon of the detail and as such should have enough personnel to cover all arcs through a complete 360 degrees with the Principal and PPO within.

Unfortunately and more often than not the deciding factor on team strength is how much the Principal / Client is willing to pay and as such a PES can quite often be just one individual, if in fact there is a PES at all.

If operating as a Hostile Environment PPO you will often have a sizeable PES in operation, due to the threat level.

Equipment

- Primary form of communication (radio transceiver plus batteries to last duration of mission)
- Secondary form of communication - in a hostile environment role this is often an alternate band transceiver, transponder, satellite phone or cell phone.
- Principal's itinerary
- Mapping
- Air photographs / satellite imagery
- Correct documentation for move (passports, visas, international drivers licence, weapons documents, vehicle documents, etc.)

NOTES

4.2
Walking Drills

Low Profile
- No 'set piece' formations
- PES and PPO positions are fluid dependent on surroundings and situation.
- PPO should remain in close proximity to the Principal at all times.
- For the PPO, adopting a position to the immediate left or right of the Principal is often favourable, giving the impression of a colleague or friend.
- Poor drills can have a detrimental effect on the Principal's image.
- Effective all round protection should be maintained at all times in line with a covert posture.
- Blend in with your surroundings.

High Profile
- High Profile walking drills can deter hostile action but can also draw unwanted attention.
- Positions are not fixed.
- PES members should alter their position to suit the surroundings and position of the Principal.

Formation Guidelines
- The following examples serve as a guide and are designed on the assumption that the PPO is right-handed.
- Left-handed PPOs should adopt the opposite side: this includes PES positions.
- The PPO's position is not fixed but is adjusted according to the direction of threat.
- Some positions work better than others.
- Adapt the formations to suit the situation.

NOTES

Example Formations

PPO only

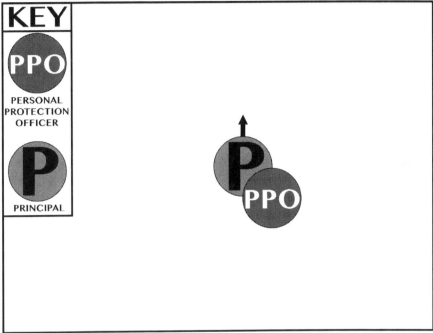

Figure 2: The PPO positions himself to the left or right but slightly to the rear of the Principal. In this case the PPO is right-handed and as such positions himself slightly right. The PPO can also switch position around the Principal as situations develop or at the appearance of a threat.

NOTES

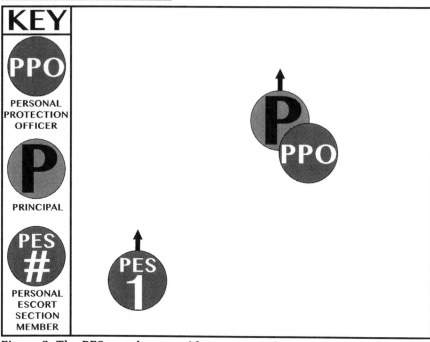

Figure 3: The PES member provides an extra element of protection to the rear or anywhere deemed necessary.

NOTES

PPO + 1 PES member Example 2

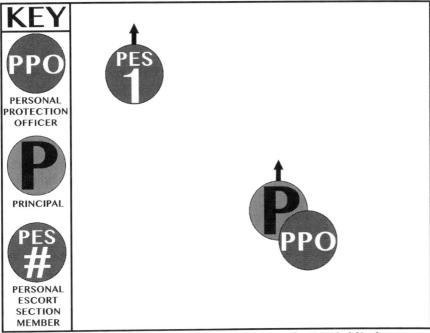

Figure 4: the PES member is positioned to cover the PPO's blind spot (caused by the Principal)

NOTES

55

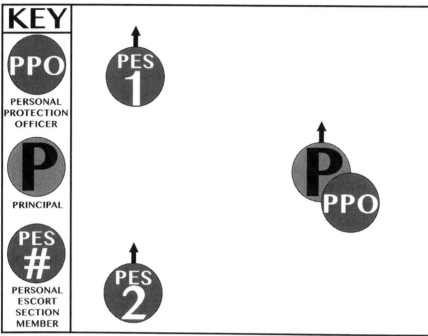

Figure 5: Two PES members provide additional intimate support.

NOTES

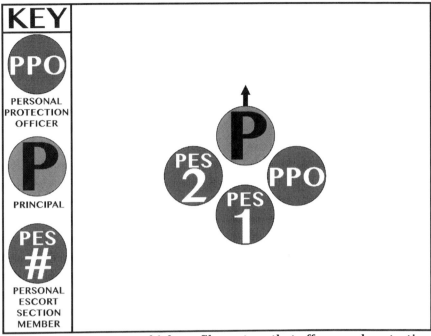

Figure 6 demonstrates a high profile posture that offers good protection in many situations but can poor for the Principal's image.

NOTES

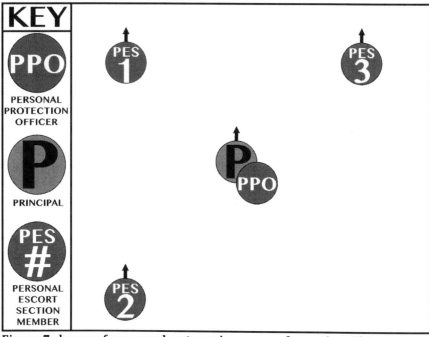

Figure 7 shows a four-member team in an open formation. This can rapidly become a closed formation as shown in the next figure.

NOTES

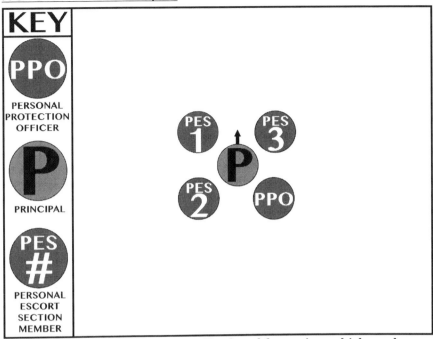

Figure 8 demonstrates a high profile closed formation, which can be augmented by a fifth member, shown in the following figures.

NOTES

PPO + 4 PES members Example 1

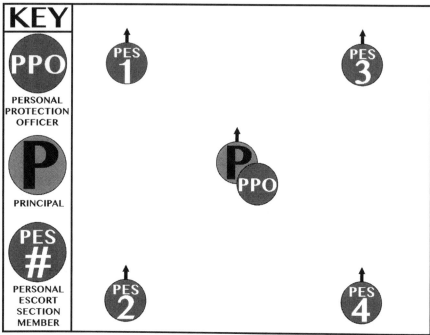

Figure 9 demonstrates a team strength of five in an open formation.

NOTES

PPO + 4 PES members Example 2

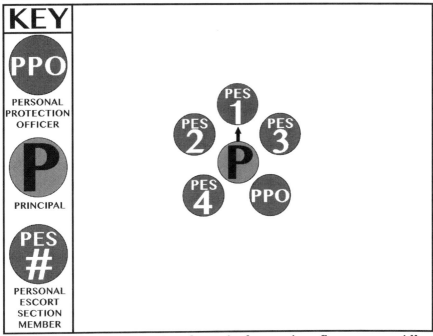

Figure 10: the open formation shown in the previous figure can rapidly become a tight defence as shown here.

NOTES

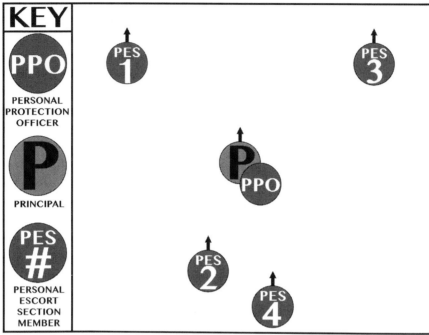

Figure 11: one of many alternatives to the "box" formation. The team should adapt their positions to suit the situation and environment.

NOTES

PPO + 4 PES Split

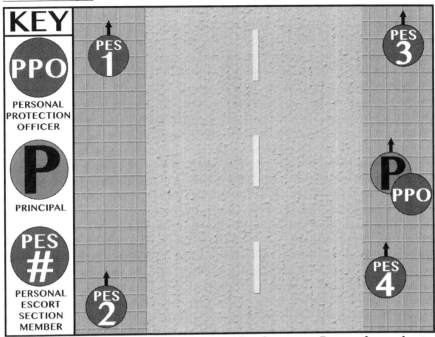

Figure 12 shows a PES split on either side of a street. Remember, adapt to suit the surroundings and constantly reassess the situation to place yourself in the best possible position to provide effective security.

NOTES

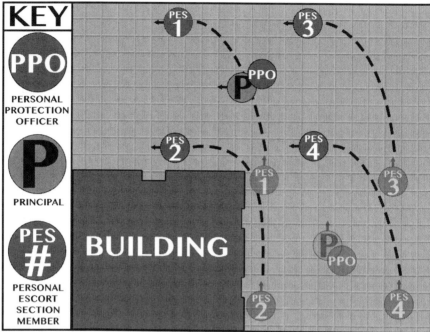

Figure 13: this diagram illustrates the positions of the PES before and after a left-hand direction change. PES members do not "wheel" with the Principal. Instead, they simply re-orientate to the new direction of travel. Note that before the turn PES 1+3 are the forward members. After the turn the forward members become PES 1+2.

NOTES

4.3
Foot Move - Immediate Action (Actions On)

Foot Immediate Action Principles - ABC SIR.:
- A - Aggressive Action
- B - Body Cover
- C - Coordination
- S - Safe Haven
- I - Initiative
- R - Rehearsals

AGGRESSIVE ACTION - Be as aggressive as the situation requires. Failure to act forcefully enough will result in loss of the initiative and control of the Principal. However, an over zealous reaction to a situation could result in embarrassment of the Principal.

BODY COVER - This speaks for itself - provide the Principal with adequate, effective body cover. Utilise extra members of the team if the situation requires and allows.

COORDINATION - Whether operating as a single PPO or fortunate enough to have a PES to bolster the team, all parties should be thoroughly coordinated in the event of an incident. Being completely aware of your surroundings at all times and conducting dynamic threat assessments on the move will aid personal and team coordination, ensuring a swift immediate action and subsequent extraction.

SAFE HAVEN - Safe havens should have already been identified during the planning cycle - but you should constantly reassess their suitability on the move and select additional safe havens as required.

INITIATIVE - The aggressor will invariably choose ground advantageous to him. He may have the element of surprise (although Cooper's Colour Codes can help prevent this) and as such they will have the initiative at the onset of an incident. The sooner the team regains the initiative, the more chance the team has of repelling and/or evading an attack. Fast aggressive action decided by a dynamic threat assessment is key.

REHEARSALS - YOU MUST conduct effective, frequent training of individual and team skills and immediate actions drills. YOU MUST conduct realistic test exercises confirming immediate action drills, also testing actions on for extra ordinary occurrences. Failure to conduct effective rehearsals will result in a sub standard response to an incident / aggressor.

Foot IA Guidelines and Examples

Members of the team should not get involved in disrupting a threat if other members have already reacted effectively - protection of the Principal is paramount. Over commitment by PES members will reduce the team's effectiveness.

Long-range attacks are considered those to which little physical disruption to the threat can be made (e.g. sniper; mortar; thrown missile).In this case body cover is almost always the only action, followed by evacuation. However, the PES / PPO may be able to disrupt the attacker dependent on the situation and environment e.g. armed assignments.

Short-range attacks can be considered those situations in which, if required, a physical reaction by the security detail can disrupt the attacker (e.g. unarmed attacks; knives; short range ballistic weapons such as pistols).

Body cover - if the Principal is between the PPO and the attacker, such as the examples shown below, the two positions must be immediately reversed in order to provide appropriate body cover.

Verbally and physically control the Principal, loud verbal commands coupled with strong physical movements. Put the Principal where you need him.

If the PES or PPO engages the attacker in any manner it is to be done aggressively.

When evacuating the Principal, any members of the PES not involved in disrupting the attacker should provide additional body cover to the Principal.

NOTES

IA Unarmed PPO + 2 PES Example 1

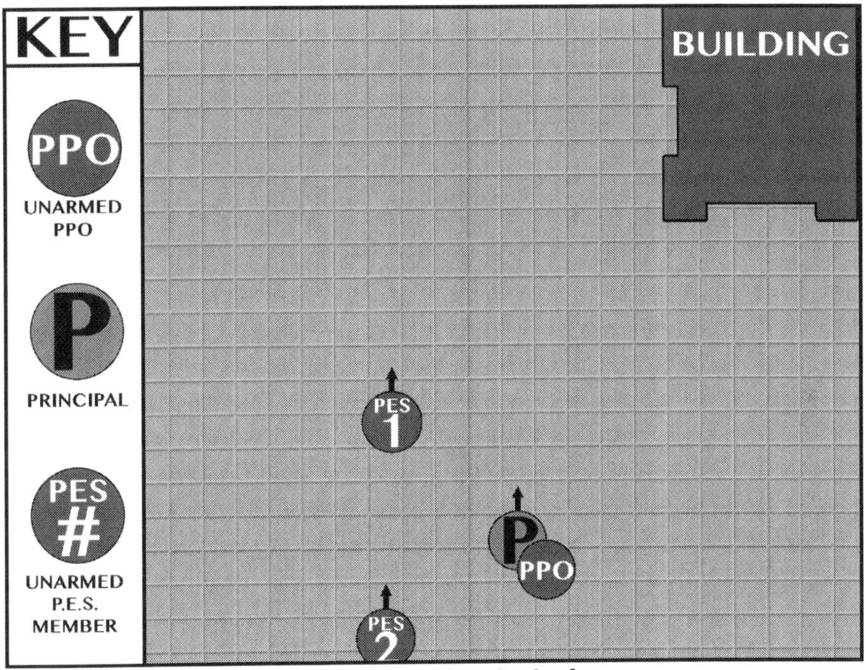

Figure 14: Unarmed team moving with Principal

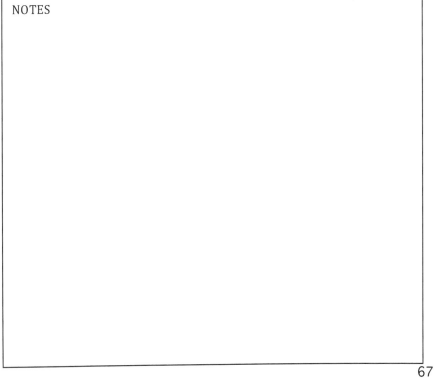

NOTES

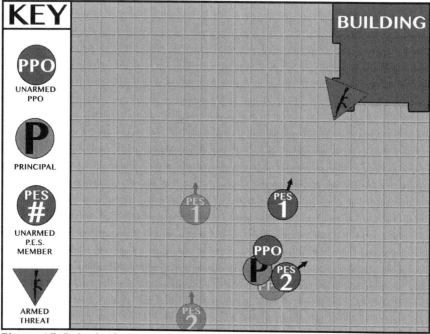

Figure 15: Principal attacked from the front by an armed assailant. PES 2 moves to augment the PPO's body cover of the Principal. PES 1 moves directly into the attacker's line of fire to reduce the attacker's field of view / fire. The PPO places himself between the attacker and the Principal, controlling the Principal and providing body cover.

NOTES

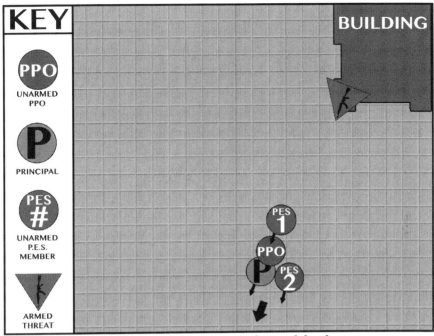

Figure 16: The team evacuate the Principal out of the danger area, preferably to a safe haven or team vehicle.

NOTES

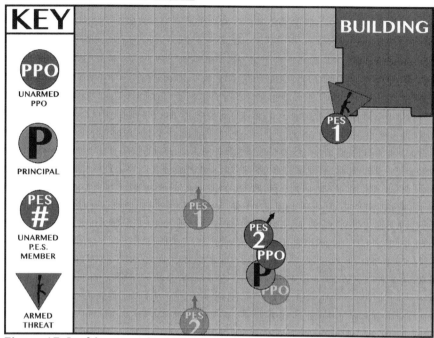

Figure 17: In this example, PES 1 feels he is close enough to physically disrupt the attacker. Simultaneously, the PPO and PES 2 move to provide body cover to the Principal and prepare to extract if necessary.

NOTES

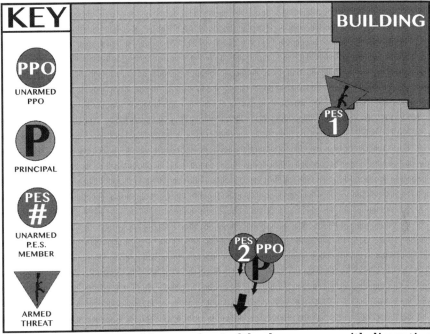

Figure 18: The Principal is moved out of the danger area with disruption to the attacker by PES 1 and body cover from the PPO and PES 2.

NOTES

71

IA Armed PPO + 4 PES Example

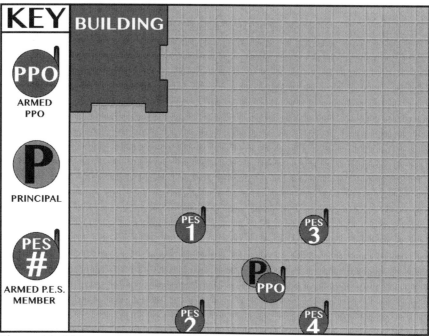

Figure 19: PPO + 4 man armed PES escort the Principal

NOTES

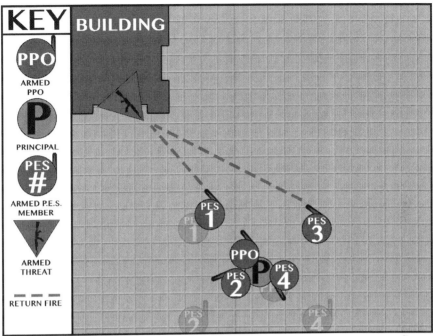

Figure 20: The Principal is attacked from the front. PES 1+3 return fire: note PES 1 moves into the line of fire to reduce the attacker's field of fire / view. Concurrently, the PPO and PES' 2+4 move to provide body cover to the Principal.

NOTES

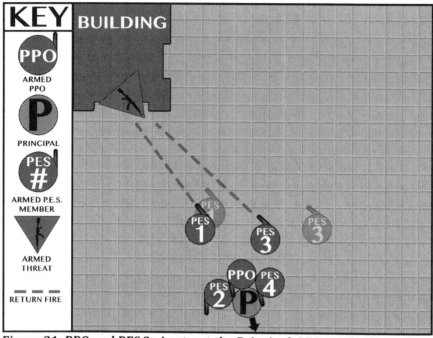

Figure 21: PPO and PES 2+4 extract the Principal. PES 1+3 facilitate the extraction using fire and maneuver rearwards, to a) continue suppression of the attacker if necessary and b) remain close enough to the Principal to provide support in the event of a secondary attack.

NOTES

Section 5
Vehicle Moves

5.1
Route Selection, Recce and Planning

- Avoid routine - all aspects.
- Insist on accurate timings.
- Select a route that allows the maximum safe speed (N.b. shortest is not always safest).
- Apply the 'need to know' principle.
- Select suitable vehicle for the journey.
- Plan alternative routes.
- Have sufficient men and vehicles for the task - if you can spare the men and vehicles, use all vehicles that will be used on the day as it gives people an opportunity to appreciate any problem areas with regard to convoy control.

Route Recce

To be conducted on same day/time of planned journey where possible.

Recce report to include:
- Location, date, time, city, state, and country
- Departure/arrival point, and time of movement
- Type of movement:
- Single vehicle / multi-vehicle?
- With escort?
- Streets and highways to be travelled
- Road condition (surface type and condition)
- Daily traffic flow (light, moderate, heavy)
- Time
- Holiday and weekend traffic flow (light, moderate, heavy)
- Bridges that open for waterway traffic
- Flyovers
- Can things be dropped on the route from above (locations)
- Railroad tracks and tunnels
- High ground, culverts, crossings
- Buildings along route
- School zones
- Road construction zones
- What do detour signs look like
- Special events (parades, sporting events, concerts etc.)
- Traffic lights and stop signs along route
- Hospitals, police stations, fire stations, emergency response units.
- Emergency response times.

- Has a secondary route been surveyed [always]
- Have safe havens been designated [always]
- Have route checkpoints been selected and codes assigned if necessary
- Will a counter surveillance team be used?

5.2
Vulnerable Points and Route Cards

A vulnerable point (VP) can be considered as any area that causes the team to alter their speed, direction of travel or formation at a location that also provides good insertion/extraction routes, cover or other advantages to hostile parties.

Some Examples of Vulnerable Points

- Junctions and Roundabouts
- Pedestrian Crossings
- Dimly lit areas
- Low ground with high surrounding structures or features
- Tunnels / Bridges
- Heavy Foliage
- Acute Inclines / Declines
- Hazardous Material areas (Petrol stations, gas works etc.)
- One-way streets
- Heavy Congestion

Route Cards

A route card is a text-based representation of the complete journey, broken down into legs, each leg showing specific information. A route card should always be completed as part of the planning process. It allows accurate time appreciation on the move and prediction of early or late arrival at the destination.

For return journeys, route cards should be prepared for both the route out and the route in i.e. to the venue and back.

NOTES

Route Card Example

The following route card is for a spotted route, where spots have been allocated for key points on the journey. Spots can also be used to break down particularly long legs. Spotting allows for simple Command, Control and Communication.

In this example:

- C1 = Principal's hotel
- Green 1 = Prominent road junction
- Green 2 = Prominent road junction
- C4 = Venue

Leg	Time	From	To	Time Taken (min)	Distance (miles)	Speed (mph)	Safe Havens	Vulnerable Points
1	0	C2	Green 1	1.5	0.6	24	Quay Hotel	Second roundabout
2	1:30	Green 1	Green 2	2.75	1.8	39	Quay Hotel	Drury Lane
3	4:15	Green 2	C4	3.50	3.2	55	Tesco Retail	Nil
TOTAL TIME			7m 45s		TOTAL DISTANCE	5.6miles		

NOTES

5.3
Vehicle Pre-Deployment Checks and Equipment

Vehicle Pre-deployment Checks

- Conduct a thorough search of the vehicle ensuring it has no devices attached or been tampered with. Ensure you check all parts of the vehicle:
    - The first stage of a search should be purely visual, looking at the vehicle and surrounding area for signs of tampering.
    - Take great care opening doors, flaps and lids. Think: booby trap.
    - Check the exterior including undercarriage, bumper / fender compartments, fuel cap, spare tire, all recesses.
    - Check the engine compartment including all recesses and reservoirs
    - Check the luggage compartment (boot)
    - Check the interior including all seats, partitions, door cards, roof lining.
- Once the check is complete ensure you have a full tank.
- Check other fluid levels including steering, brake and radiator.
- Check all lights are functional, interior and exterior.
- Check vehicle communications are working, check in with the Ops room or a team member to confirm.
- Initiate GPS tracking systems; acquire a fix.
- If cameras are fitted check they are functioning and have sufficient memory space to record the duration of the mission.

NOTES

Vehicle Equipment

The following equipment is a suggested kit list, which should be carried as part of your vehicle equipment.

- Spare tire (complete jack set)
- Jump start cables – (thick/heavy duty type)
- Radios, spare radios, and batteries
- Mobile phone with spare batteries/car charger
- Fire extinguisher
- Medical kit / Trauma Bag (Including any medication needed by Principal)
- Torch and spare batteries
- Spare sets of car keys
- Maps relevant to area
- Sat Nav / GPS
- Local currency and coins
- Tow chain or rope
- Umbrella
- Blankets/sleeping bags
- Drinking water x 4litres (min)
- Tissue x 4pks (min)
- Hand wash x 2 (min)
- Windscreen washer fluid
- Oil and other lubricants [correct type for vehicle]
- Telescopic search mirror
- Spare fuses, hoses, electrical tape, bulbs
- Towels and hand towels, rags, overalls
- Comms information (Contact lists, frequencies etc.)
- Tyre pressure gauge
- Window hammer
- Fuel card
- Warning triangle
- Vehicle documents (Logbook, insurance certificate, vehicle manual etc.)
- Emergency food.
- Seat belt cutters
- On-board cameras (e.g. Roadhawk)
- Compact camera (hand held)

NOTES

Hostile Environment / Extreme Climate Eqpt.

Other recommended equipment, which may be carried when working in an extreme climate or hostile environment –

- Sledgehammer and crowbar
- Bolt cutters
- Respirators
- Smoke hoods
- Protective suits
- Spade
- Snow shovel
- Snow chains
- Ice scraper / De-icer
- Sand plates
- Cat litter (absorbent)
- Coverall
- Latex gloves
- Hand held metal detectors
- Portable oxygen equipment
- Body armor
- Backup weapons and ammo
- Spare fuel
- Flares
- Winch
- Front nudge bar
- Vehicle Snorkel
- Identifying markings or flag.
- Movement letters or other permits required for provincial / territorial border crossings.

NOTES

5.4
Driver Protocol and Embus / Debus Procedures

Driver Protocol

- Fuel tank should be full prior to pick-up.
- Spare keys should be carried.
- Prepare the vehicle for Principal - temperature, radio off, and daily paper on backseat.
- No personal items should be in view. Keep stowed in boot.
- Driver should be inside the vehicle at all times when operating as part of the team.
- Driver should know all vehicle controls
- Apply locks once all passengers are in vehicle
- Ensure seatbelts are worn.
- Obey all traffic laws.
- Do not use horn unless it is an emergency situation.
- No smoking or eating in the Principals car at any time.
- Do not use strong scented aftershave.
- Speak when spoken to, not before.
- Driver must remain with the vehicle at all times unless instructed otherwise
- The driver must be briefed and trained on all vehicle drills and actions on.
- Driver should adhere to the dress code given by the TL or Principal.
- Snacks, refreshments and hand wipes stocked, as per the Principal's tastes.

NOTES

Embus / Debus Procedures

- Positions are dependent upon which side of the road you are driving on (left-hand traffic or right-hand traffic).
- Over 60% of the world's countries are right-hand traffic states.
- The drills shown serve as a guide. Although high profile drills are shown in the following diagrams, teams can adapt them to be low profile simply by being more discreet during the operation to avoid unnecessary attention.
- Always leave maneuvering space between cars. Never put the Principal's vehicle in a position too close to another vehicle or obstacle that it cannot maneuver if necessary.
- The Principal should sit behind the PPO but this may not always be the case. The Principal's personal preference may take over, in which case adapt the drills to suit the situation.
- Don't rush procedures - transition from vehicle to foot / foot to vehicle should still be swift with Principal exposure kept to a minimum.
- Principle should not move until all members of team in place but he should not be delayed either - passage of information and good command + control (C2) will facilitate a smooth transition.
- The Principal's vehicle should get as close to the entrance / exit of the venue as possible (where possible, the SAP team can secure a parking space for Principal's vehicle prior to arrival - covertly)
- Try and ensure the Principal will not be required to cross streets / traffic during the transition.
- Drivers stay behind the wheel, engines on, in-gear ready to move upon incident and alert to the environment around him, scanning for threats.
- Doors are not unlocked or opened until last safe moment.
- During a debus the Principal's door should not be closed until the Principal is safely in the venue.
- Always try and achieve an orthodox embus / debus.

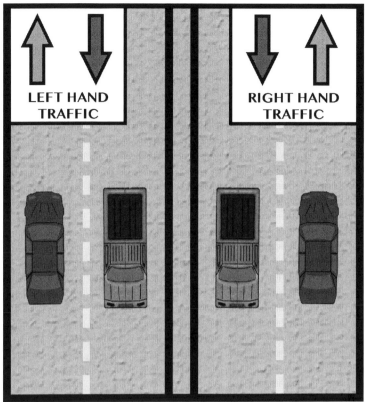

Figure 22: The traffic keys displayed in the top left and top right of this image are used in this section.

Left hand drive countries include the United Kingdom, Japan, Australia, Cyprus and India.

Right hand drive countries include the United States of America, Canada, Brazil, Germany, China, Holland.

LHT Orthodox Debus

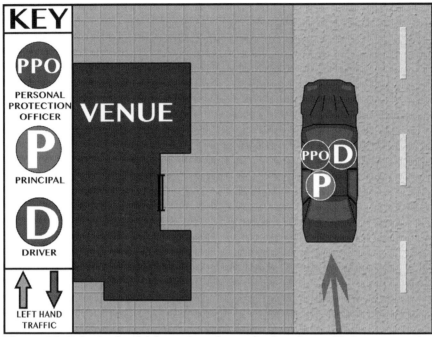

Figure 23: Principal vehicle arrives for orthodox drop off; doors remain locked until the last safe moment. The Driver positions the car so that the Principal's door is adjacent to the entrance.

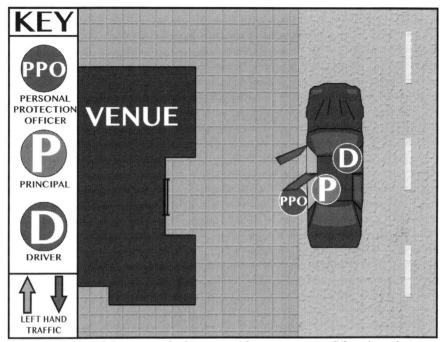

Figure 24: PPO debuses and after a rapid assessment of the situation opens the Principal's door.

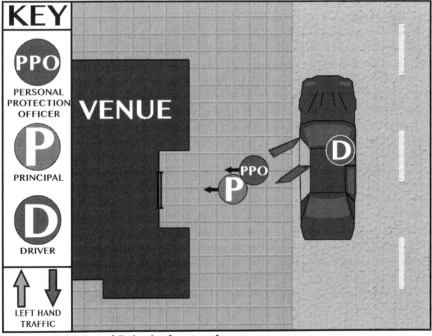

Figure 25: PPO and Principal enter the venue.

LHT Unorthodox Debus

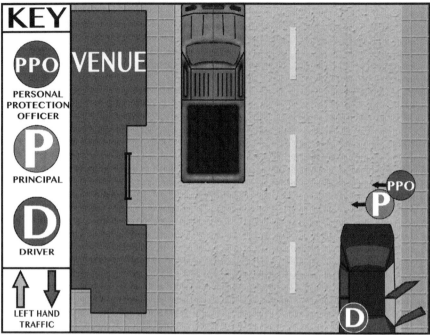

Figure 26: Vehicle halts for unorthodox drop off; doors are unlocked at last safe moment. The Driver positions the car so that its rear is adjacent to the venue entrance.

NOTES

RHT Orthodox Debus

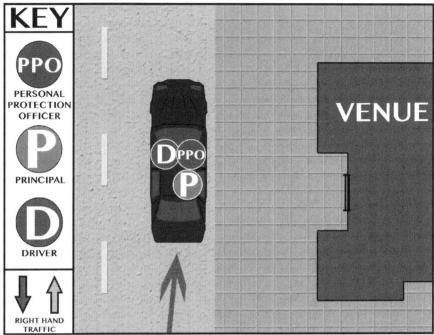

Figure 27: RIGHT HAND TRAFFIC, E.g. USA / Canada. Principal vehicle arrives for orthodox drop off; doors remain locked until the last safe moment. The Driver positions the car so that the Principal's door is adjacent to the venue entrance.

NOTES

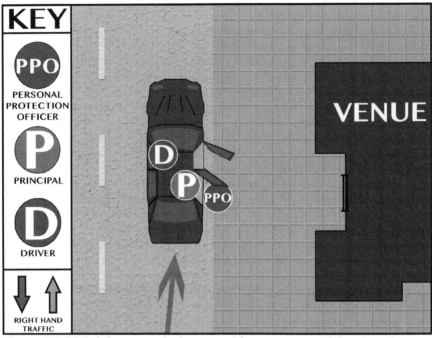

Figure 28: PPO debuses and after a rapid assessment of the situation opens the Principal's door.

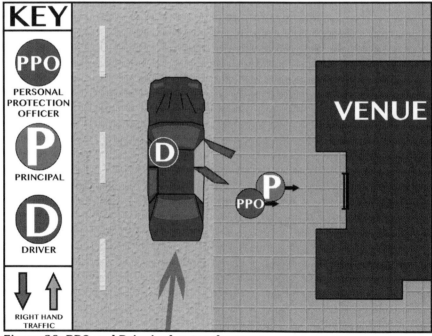

Figure 29: PPO and Principal enter the venue.

RHT Unorthodox debus

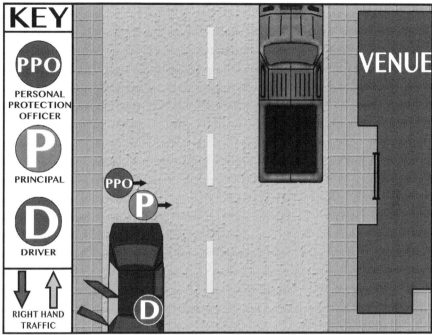

Figure 30: Unorthodox debus involving street crossing with the PPO and Principal immediately at curbside when stopping. The Driver positions the car so that its rear is adjacent to the venue entrance.

Embus Procedures

- Embus procedures are essentially the debus procedures in reverse. The same basic principals apply.
- Remember that on an orthodox embus / debus; the Principal's door should be level with the venue exit point.
- An unorthodox embus / debus should see the rear of the Principal's vehicle level with the venue exit point.

NOTES

5.5
Vehicle Formations and Actions On

Vehicle Formations - Points to Note

The following graphical representations depict only two vehicles (Principal + PES Backing Car) although more vehicles may be part of the team. The position of the backing vehicle relative to the Principal's vehicle is crucial to provide adequate intimate security and immediate reaction on the move.

Remember:

- Drive at the maximum safe speed for the weather, road condition, driver's ability and the legal limit.
- The backing vehicle must always be in a suitable position to provide an effective response when required.
- Driver protocol and skills must be of the highest standard, not only to respond effectively in emergency situations but also to prevent compromise or embarrassment of the Principal and the team. Don't create accidents through erratic driving.
- Preempt upcoming hazards: junctions, corners, roundabouts, motorway entry / exits, traffic control systems and other areas identified by the Security Advance Party and detailed in the Route Card.
- The Principal's driver and backing vehicle driver must position their vehicles in such a way to aid observation and defence. To that end both drivers must be acutely aware of the location of the other. Simple adjustments to exploit full use of the road width can significantly enhance the defensive capability of a convoy. The backing vehicle must be able to see ahead of the Principal's vehicle.
- On embus and debus the back up driver should ensure the front wheels are directed away from the principal and their vehicle. This is to stop the backup vehicle crashing into the principal or their vehicle if they are rammed into from behind.

NOTES

Departing

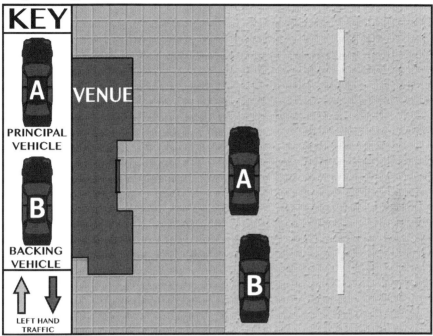

Figure 31: The Principal is inside his vehicle and the callsign prepares to move. N.b. the backing vehicle is parked slightly offset to the Principal vehicle, acting as a block and increasing its field of view to the front.

NOTES

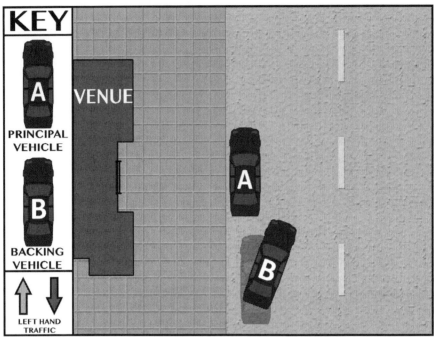

Figure 32: The backing vehicle moves first, edging out into the road - providing a block to a) protect the Principal vehicle in the event of an ram attack from the rear and b) allow the Principal vehicle clear access into the road.

NOTES

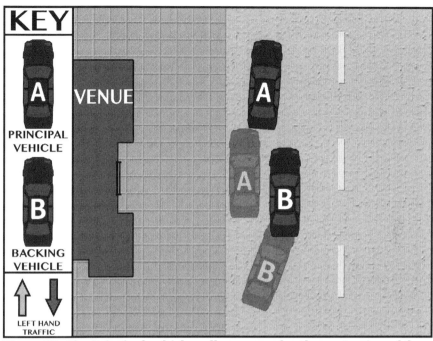

Figure 33: The Principal vehicle pulls away under the protection of the backing vehicle, which immediately falls into formation.

NOTES

Junctions

LHT Junction Exit

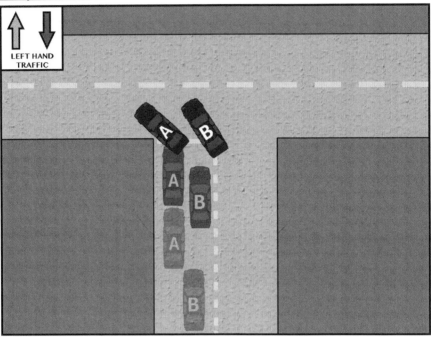

Figure 34 - Exiting a junction, the PES vehicle provides a rolling defensive block to oncoming traffic.

NOTES

RHT Junction Exit

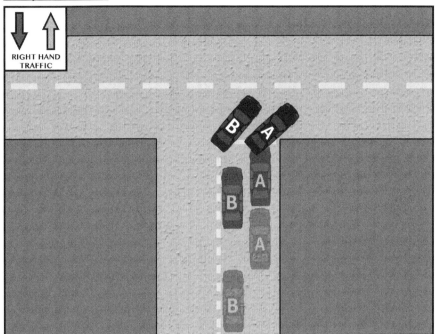

Figure 35: Exiting a junction, the PES vehicle provides a rolling defensive block to on coming traffic.

N.b. Crossing lanes of opposing traffic

Crossing lanes of opposing traffic (such as turning left instead of right in the Figure 25) should be avoided where at all possible Select routes during planning to avid such instances. However, scenarios will invariably occur where crossing lanes is unavoidable. In this case, the backing vehicle should provide a block to the flank, which the Vehicle Commander deems to be the highest threat.

NOTES

Roundabouts (Traffic Circles)

LHT Roundabout, 1st Exit

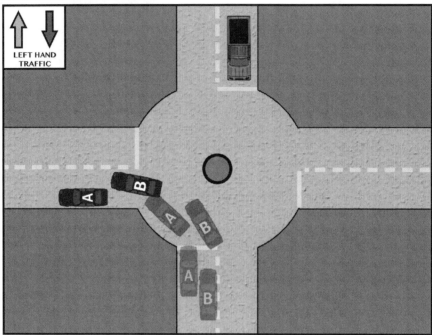

Figure 36: The backing vehicle provides a rolling block to the right (the direction of oncoming traffic)

NOTES

LHT Roundabout, Other exits

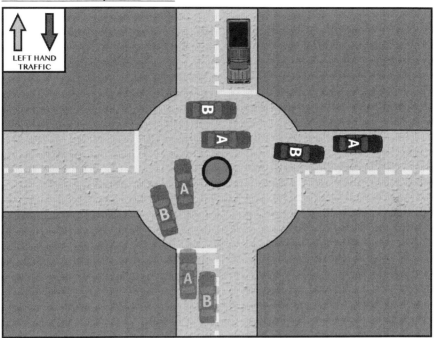

Figure 37: The backing vehicle provides a rolling block to the right on entry and subsequently to the left as the principal's vehicle passes other entry points onto the roundabout.

NOTES

RHT Roundabout, 1st Exit

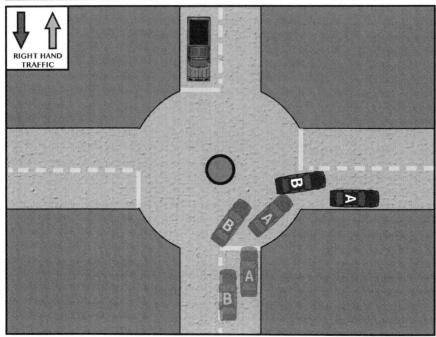

Figure 38: The backing vehicle provides a rolling block to the left (the direction of oncoming traffic)

NOTES

RHT Roundabout, Other exits

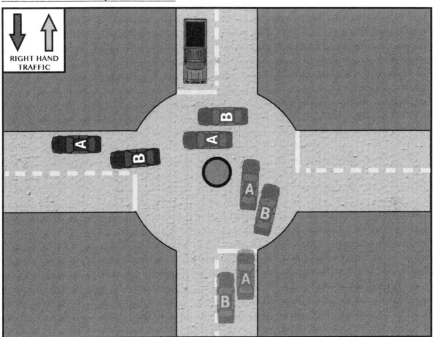

Figure 39: The backing vehicle provides a rolling block to the left on entry and subsequently to the right as the principal's vehicle passes other entry points onto the roundabout.

NOTES

Bends

LHT Bend

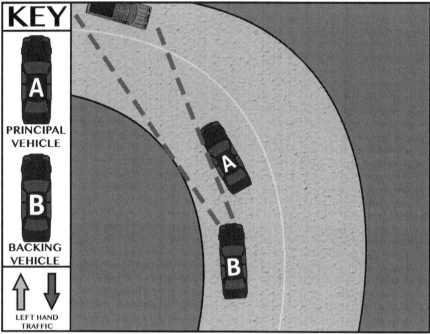

Figure 40: Backing vehicle positioned for a blind bend, allowing maximum view to the front.

NOTES

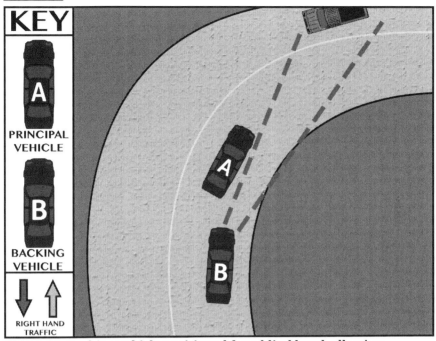

Figure 41: Backing vehicle positioned for a blind bend, allowing maximum view to the front.

NOTES

Motorways (Highways)

LHT Motorway cruising positions

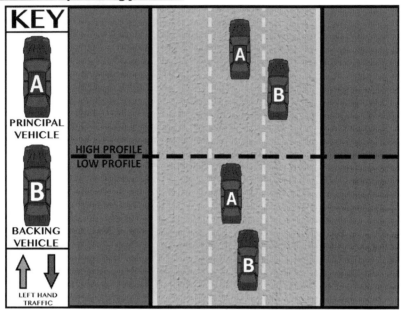

Figure 42: Cruising positions, low and high profile, left-hand traffic

LHT Motorway merging

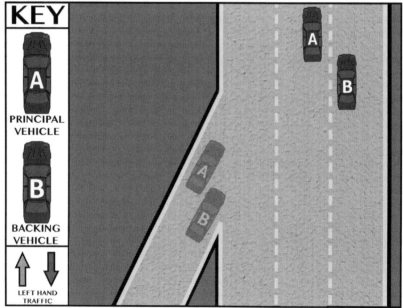

Figure 43: The PES vehicles blocks to the side of oncoming traffic.

LHT Motorway exit

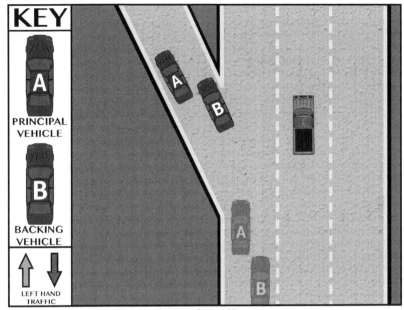

Figure 44: Motorway Exit Left-Hand Traffic

RHT Motorway cruising positions

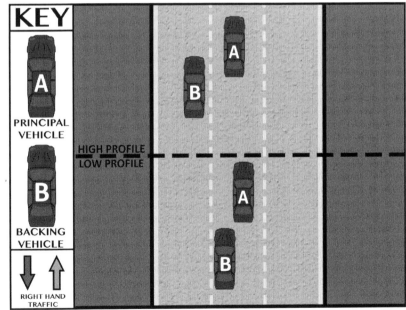

Figure 45: Cruising positions, low and high profile, right-hand traffic

RHT Motorway merging

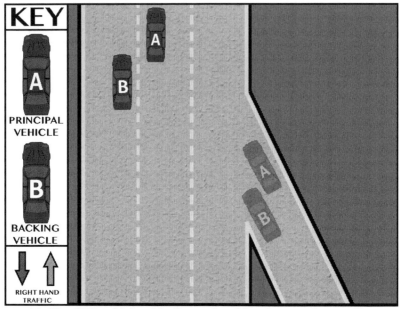

Figure 46: The PES vehicles blocks to the side of oncoming traffic.

RHT Motorway exit

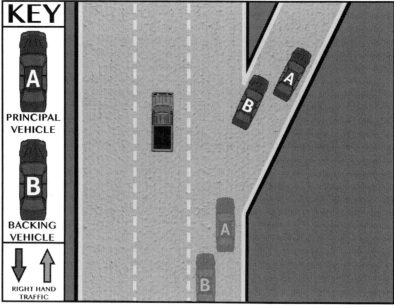

Figure 47: Motorway Exit Right-Hand Traffic

Lane Changes

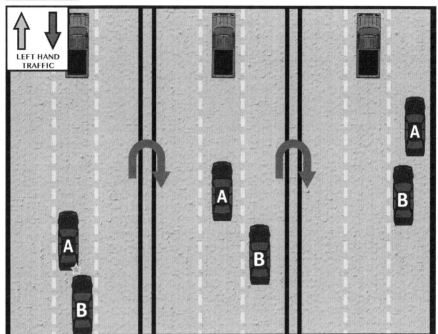

Figure 48:

-As early as possible, the Principal's driver identifies the need to change lanes and when ready, signals with indicator lights the intention to change lanes.

-The backing PES vehicle observes the signal and moves into the intended lane when suitable.

-Only after the PES vehicle is in the intended lane does the Principal's vehicle change lanes.

N.b. The signal from the Alpha's indicator lights should not be kept flashing as would be normal procedure for general, civilian style driving. Instead, the indicator light is flashed only twice, this is enough for the backing vehicle driver to identify it but not to telegraph the move. It also dismisses the requirement for radio communication between vehicles.

NOTES

5.6
Immediate Action

Vehicle Move - Immediate Action Principles
Remembered using the mnemonic CARCASS

Coordination must be up and down the Chain of Command, as well as laterally between all team members and of course the Principal – before, during and after a mission or incident. The team members must know the situation at all times. The impact of good or bad coordination is directly relative to the number of operators and vehicles on the ground. All information relating to mobility/effectiveness of the team and enemy must be relayed immediately whether in Contact or not.

Analysis / Anticipation:
- ANALYSIS - As part of mission planning a recce should always be conducted on the route. At minimum a map recce, but best case is a physical reconnaissance by team members. Early identification of Key Terrain and Vulnerable Points is vital in order to identify likely ambush locations.

- ANTICIPATION does not imply the need for a tense operator expecting an attack at every corner. Instead, it requires that an operator is Situation Aware, reading the combat indicators and using this information to make dynamic assessments on the move. This heightened awareness is invaluable to the PES.

Remember that at the time of springing, the ambush party is at a significant advantage over their target due to the element of surprise and their weight of fire. The first few seconds will dictate who is likely to win or lose and as such anticipation is key to successful protection of the Principal.

Rehearsals: Thorough rehearsals will enable the team to adapt the drills more effectively when under duress. Rehearsals will also allow the team to employ early alterations to SOPs depending on the information gained on recce.

Where possible, encourage the Principal to partake in rehearsals but not so much as to turn him into a bag of nerves. Rehearsals should be conducted in full kit and equipment and using the vehicles that will be used for the mission, or the closest make / model / specification available.

Communication: Simple and effective comms procedures should be employed and rehearsed thoroughly. The importance of effective comms between team members/vehicles cannot be emphasised enough – passage of information is vital to effective coordination, increased situational awareness and anticipation of the attack. Ensure backup systems are employed for technical equipment (HF/VHF/GSM).If employing vehicle horns keep signals simple and short. Be aware that with armored vehicles this will often be difficult to hear. Have hand signals prepared as a last resort or to augment other methods of communication. Multiple signals for Contact should be identified and used in an incident. Small arms fire is difficult to hear inside an armored vehicle unless the vehicle itself is being struck. The more signals you can employ immediately and without hampering your immediate action, the sooner the rest of the call sign can respond and adapt to the information being passed.

Adaptability: There are only so many scenarios you can rehearse for before running the risk of information overload or confusion within the team. Keep drills basic but know them intimately. Know when and where adaptations can take place and what factors must be considered to adapt effectively. The element of surprise is the enemy's best tool; as a result they will constantly try new and innovative ways to initiate an attack. The team's ability to adjust to this initiation and respond effectively is paramount to the safeguarding of the Principal.

Situational Awareness: The term Situational Awareness relates to the team's awareness in general and detail. For example, general awareness may include some of the following information: own geographical location, nearby hospitals (and facilities provided), Embassies, Police stations / checkpoints, safe havens, military checkpoints, helicopter landing sites. Awareness in detail refers to the intimate details of the team on the ground, the enemy and all other factors (fixed and variable) within the immediate locale of the team: Principal location, civilian locations, suspect vehicles / packages / possible threats, vulnerable flanks, team dispositions. Remember at all times the three-dimensional battle space. An attack cannot only launch from part of your 360-degree arc but also from above and below.
A good commentary from the lead vehicle will significantly improve the team's situational awareness and as such commentary driving should have a constant presence in the security detail's training regime.

Speed: Every action under ambush must be conducted at speed and under control. The longer it takes to respond to an attack, the longer the Principal is in the killing area and the less chance the team has of protecting him. Corners must not be cut but adaptations to suit the situation must be identified and adopted quickly.

NOTES

CASUALTIES

The following sub-sections do not provide examples with casualties in the immobilised vehicle for the simple fact that there are hundreds of possible variations.

Drills may have to be altered during the incident in the event of serious casualties in either the lead or backing vehicle.

Multiple casualties is one of few reasons that a driver should exit the vehicle.

General Cross-Decking

X-decking Points

- DRIVERS must remain in vehicles unless a mass casualty situation dictates otherwise.
- PES members should not exit vehicles unless absolutely necessary to facilitate the cross-deck.
- All team members should be familiar with all door controls and locking mechanisms on ALL vehicles in the convoy.
- During an incident the Principal may be cross-decked into any vehicle. Secondary attacks mean that cross-decking drills should be practiced on ALL convoy vehicles, not just the Principal's own vehicle.
- Poorly stowed weapons or equipment will result in slow cross-deck drills and increased exposure to the threat. Loose items such as vehicle tools or clipboards in vehicles can fatally injure occupants in an RTA or IED blast. Strap down or stow anything that would not be immediately required.
- Casualties must be identified and team notified as soon as possible as casualties may significantly affect cross-deck drills. IF POSSIBLE, conscious team members inside the affected vehicle should pass details via radio immediately "Bravo down, one casualty" - keep things simple.
- Drivers should attempt to turn broadside to the threat, providing maximum cover for cross-deck. See below.

NOTES

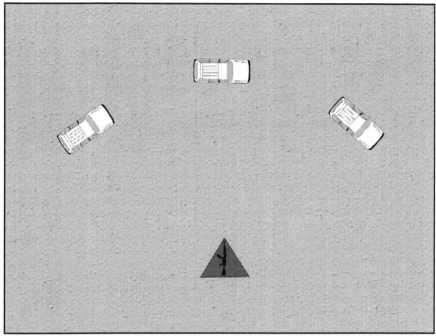

Figure 49 Turn vehicles broadside to the threat if possible. This allows exit on a "safe" side through at least two doors.

X-deck Sequence of Events

1. **Trigger:** This could be an ambush or simply a major mechanical failure that has immobilised the Principal's vehicle.
2. **Order:** Cross-deck is ordered or otherwise initiated.
3. **Move:** Vehicles move into position.
4. **Secure:** Team members secure the immediate area of the Principal's vehicle and the cross-deck vehicle - this is where the Principal will be exposed. PES members in additional convoy vehicles provide an exterior cordon.
5. **Cross-deck:** Principal is cross-decked to new vehicle.
6. **Extract:** Team extracts from the area under the guidance of the PPO or, if incapacitated, the next in command.

NOTES

X-deck Example- Two vehicle armed team

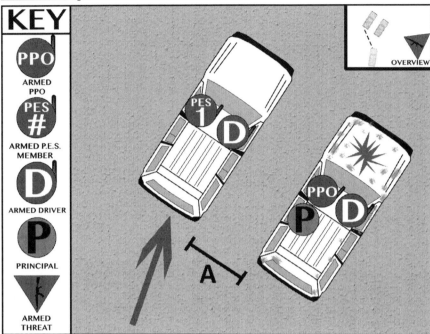

Figure 50: Principal vehicle is contacted from the right, immobilising the vehicle - prompting a cross deck. The backing vehicle pulls to the 'safe' side, using the immobilised vehicle as a shield.

IMPORTANT: It is vital that the distance at 'A' in the figure above is as narrow as possible but still allows both vehicles doors to be fully opened. Too wide a gap and the Principal will be over-exposed during cross deck. Too narrow a gap: the cross-deck will be slowed significantly due to hindrance to doors, prolonging time in the killing area.

NOTES

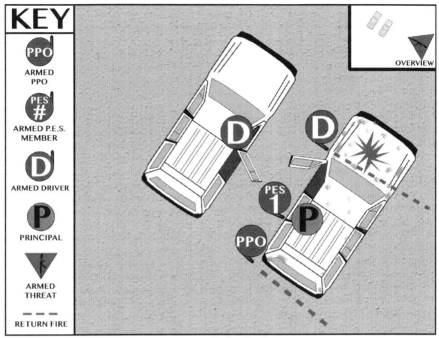

Figure 51: Team prepares to move Principal.

The PPO and Driver exit the vehicle and provide a base of fire. Concurrently, the backing Vehicle Commander (PES 1) moves to the Principal's door. To do this, PES 1 climbs through to the back of the vehicle and exits out of the rear passenger door nearest the immobilised vehicle - ensuring he leaves this door OPEN, ready to receive the Principal.

NOTES

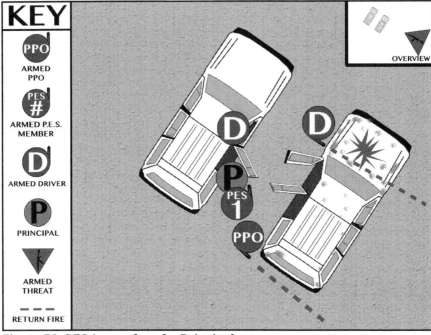

OVERVIEW

D

D

P

PES 1

PPO

Figure 52: PES 1 transfers the Principal.

The backing Vehicle Commander (PES 1) opens the Principal's door and with speed and force, moves the Principal into the backing vehicle through the passenger door he left open.

As he does this, PES 1 uses his body to shield the Principal from any incoming fire or flying debris / shrapnel. The open doors also provide a level of protection from the front of the vehicles, in case of a flank attack.

PES 1 will place the Principal into the foot well behind the front passenger seat as this is as far from the of the threat as currently possible and maintains a low posture..

NOTES

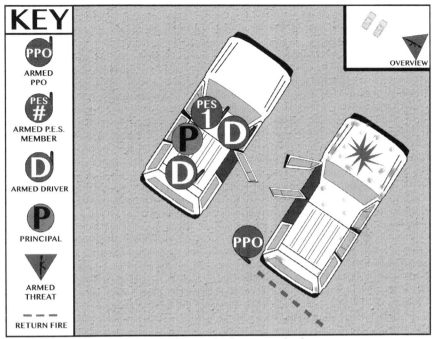

Figure 53: Driver of immobilised vehicle cross-decks.

Only once the Principal is cross-decked does the base of fire cross-deck (in this case the PPO and Driver).

The furthest member from the open door should move first - in this case the Driver. He pushes through the open doors of the immobilised vehicle and enters the backing vehicle.

As the driver enters, the Backing Vehicle Commander (PES 1) resumes his position in the front seat and the driver of the Principal's vehicle covers / controls the Principal until the arrival of the PPO).

NOTES

Figure 54: PPO enters the vehicle.

The PPO enters the vehicle and closes the door.

If this drill is carried out at speed he should be milliseconds behind the driver as he enters.

The PPO provides body cover to the Principal until out of the killing area and into a safe haven or otherwise secure.
As the vehicle evacuates, the PPO also checks the medical status of the Principal.

NOTES

Hostile Environment Considerations

- In Hostile Environments, CP / PSD teams will often consist of 3-4 vehicles, sometimes more.
- There will more than likely be several 'Clients' under the protection of the team and they will span across multiple vehicles within the team.
- The lead vehicle is generally kept empty due to the increased threat of IED attacks.
- Extra vehicles in the convoy can provide flank protection and points of fire to assist the cross-deck.

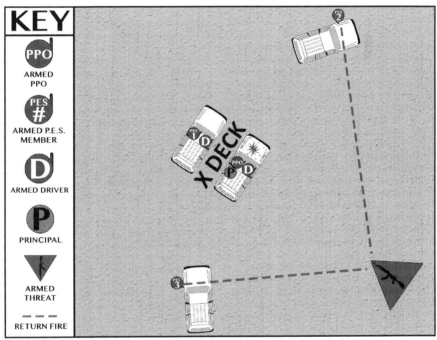

Figure 55: Flanking fire from other vehicles in a PSD team.

- Some teams may opt to slightly offset the x-decking vehicle from the immobilised vehicle as shown in the following diagram. This slight variation provides more cover to the Driver and cab area of the backing vehicle.

NOTES

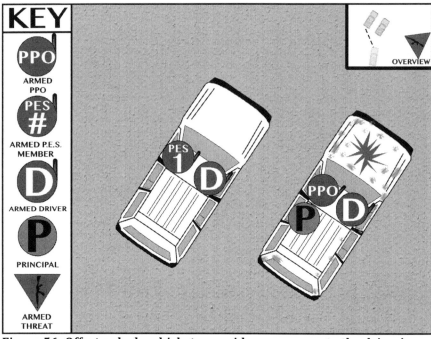

Figure 56: Offset x-deck vehicle to provide more cover to the driver's cab.

NOTES

Road Block Immediate Action

- There are predominantly three options available: 1) Extract in vehicles 2) extract on foot 3) Push through the block. 4) Cross-deck
- Road block IA depends on many factors including a callsign's proximity to the block; the type of vehicles in the callsign; the type of block - light vehicle, heavy vehicle or other obstacle; the status of vehicles in the callsign - have any been immobilised during the initiation?
- Drivers should be experienced practitioners of evasive maneuvers in order to swiftly execute a change in direction to exit the killing area. Poor drills will worsen an already difficult situation.
- Ramming roadblocks should be a last resort and will only be effective if the block is in fact moveable. Vehicles that are not armoured are vulnerable to immobilisation on impact. Vehicle airbags can be deactivated if deemed necessary and relevant to the threat.
- Drivers should pick a suitable point of the block to ram. If the block consists of light vehicles / cars, the rear of these vehicles is the lightest part and should be targeted by the driver.
- Ramming should not be done at full speed. It should bc executed in low gears, controlled and accelerating at the weak point from a short distance.

Road Block Cross-deck

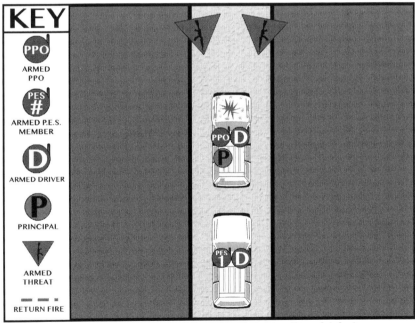

Figure 57: Roadblocked by attackers, the Principal's vehicle is immobilised in the attack.

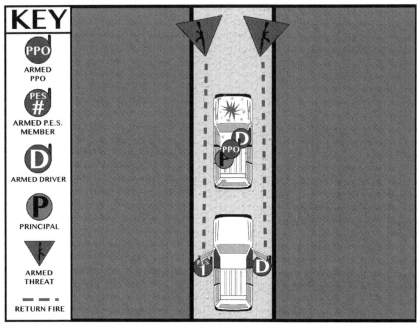

Figure 58: The PPO moves from the front seats to the back and covers the Principal, lowering his profile into the footwell or moving into the rear compartment if the tailgate (boot) is to be used to exit. The backing vehicle stops to the rear as close as possible. Both PES and Driver exit to provide a heavy weight of fire in preparation for the evacuation of the Principal.

N.b. The PES members of the backing vehicle must remain aware of the rear in order to anticipate a rear block or secondary attack. Escape routes to the flank must be identified, potentially on foot.

NOTES

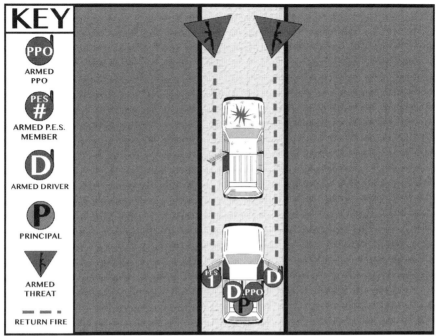

Figure 59: As the PES members open fire, the PPO, Principal and Driver exit the vehicle ensuring they leave the door OPEN to provide extra cover on the move. The Driver exits immediately behind the PPO and Principal, providing extra body cover. In some vehicles it may be more suitable / less exposed to exit through the tailgate (boot).

The PPO provides body cover to the Principal at all times, as well as verbally and physically controlling him. Upon entry into the PES vehicle the Principal is moved as far back into the vehicle and as low down as possible with the PPO and Driver providing continued body cover.

NOTES

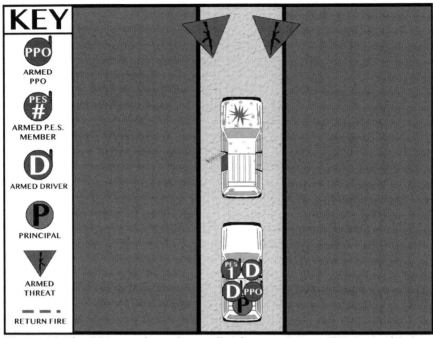

Figure 60: The PES members do not finish engaging until Principal is in the vehicle, after which point they extract rearwards.

If the rear has also been blocked, foot maneuver left or right may be required.

Other Vehicles

- Not all vehicles are primarily accessed through conventional hinged side doors. Many types of vehicle in use in the Middle East hotspots have rear doors only or sliding side doors.
- Drills must be adjusted to suit the vehicles you have in your team.

Body Cover in Vehicles

When an ambush is sprung, the PPO has two options regarding body cover:

- To direct the Principal into the foot well but remain in the front of the vehicle to provide effective Command and Control
- To move into the back of the vehicle and provide body cover to the Principal.

The choice the PPO makes is completely dependent on his perception of the situation, the nature of the threat and the capability of his Driver and team.

Controlling the Principal in Cross-deck

- In the event of a vehicle ambush the Principal is likely be in the early stages of shock or be suffering from some form of injury.
- In the event of an IED attack, this may be true for all occupants of the struck vehicle.
- Hearing will be affected, sense of direction will be affected.
- During the whole incident and cross-deck control the Principal with physical and verbal force.
- If you are the PES member cross-decking him - tell him loudly and firmly exactly what you need him to do as you move him.
- As you physically extract him from the vehicle yell "GET OUT, GET OUT"
- Outside the vehicle, cover him but do not hamper his movement - use your body as a shield and as a physical aid to move him between the vehicles.
- As you transfer him tell him "MOVE MOVE MOVE"
- As you get him into the backing vehicle tell him to "GET DOWN, GET DOWN" and continue body cover until the next team member enters the vehicle.

NOTES

Section 6
Residential Security

Basic Points

- The Residential Security Team (RST) should endeavor to permit normal routine of the household.
- Movement during silent hours should be kept to a minimum.
- Home telephone calls should be answered first by the RST.
- Doors should be answered first by the RST.
- All keys should be controlled by the RST, logging and reporting signing in / out from the key press.
- All team members should be briefed on incident Immediate Actions such as fire, attack, and medical emergency.
- All RST members should be aware of escape / evade routes.

Planning Areas

- Outer Cordon
- Intermediate Cordon (for particularly large areas)
- Inner Cordon
- Personal Cordon

NOTES

6.1
Outer Cordon

Infrastructure

- The Outer Cordon encompasses the perimeter of the grounds and its access points.
- The perimeter should have both a Primary and Secondary access point but preferably no more than two access points altogether.
- If possible, the secondary access point should allow access to and from the residence onto a different route than the primary.
- Natural protection such as existing walls, hedges and fences should be enhanced where possible to deny line of sight or physical access to the grounds.
- Access points should incorporate an airlock system if possible.
- Enhance the outer cordon with technical equipment such as CCTV.
- Logbooks should be maintained by Outer Cordon posts to record unusual activity.in the surrounding area and neighbouring homes.

Deliveries and Visitors

- All visitors should be identified and logged including vehicle and load details.
- Unexpected visitors should not be permitted access until confirmation has been received from the Ops Room.
- Deliveries should by appointment only and upon arrival should be checked against the order.
- Deliverymen should be accompanied at all times within the residence.
- Mail should be received at the Outer Cordon - deliveries should not deliver it the residence themselves.
- Changes in regular deliverymen should be checked with the company before admittance / acceptance of delivery.
- All mail and deliveries should be logged.

NOTES

Unwanted Visitors

- Interview the individual in a secure location.
- Always assume the individual may be dangerous.
- How is the person dressed
  - Business or casual clothing
  - Dirty clothing
  - Worn clothing
  - Mixed or matched clothing
  - Footwear
- What is their appearance/description (see Person Description Crib card in Section 9)
- Biographical information obtained during the interview
  - Name
  - Where from
  - How did they get to your location
  - Are they alone
- Is the visitor known by the Principal
- Be polite.
- Examine identification
- Allow individual to talk freely - this will reveal more info.
- Sample questions
  - Why do you feel this way?
  - What does this mean to you?
  - Who else have you contacted about this?
  - What response have you gotten?
  - If Principal cannot help you, what will you do?
- Watch for evasive answers, signs of anger, and non-verbal communication such as hand and body movements.
- Know local law regarding threats, mentally ill commitment, and restraining orders.
- Follow up process
  - With local law enforcement
  - With mental institutions
  - With friends, relatives, previous people contacted by the individual
  - Obtain a recent photograph
  - Maintain a file on these types of individuals
- Communicate to remainder of team and other staff details about the encounter. Brief the Principal as appropriate.

6.2
Intermediate Cordon

Infrastructure

- Secured by technical aids and a physical security presence such as roaming patrols, static posts and motion detectors or CCTV.
- Area must be well kept and well lit to deny hiding places and covert movement to intruders.
- Visitor parking areas should not be sited in close proximity to the building or external communal areas such as children's play areas.
- Lay gravel and speed humps to the driveway.
- Light the outside of the house and blind spots inwards from perimeter.
- Illuminate any CCTV blind spots.

NOTES

6.3
Inner Cordon

Infrastructure

- A zoned alarm system should be fitted and linked with local security services.
- Incorporate an airlock system on access points.
- All doors and windows should be of high quality with suitable locking systems. This includes skylights and manholes.
- Windows should be reinforced / blast proof.
- Should include a 24hr-manned Ops Room (Ops Room equipment in Section 2.4).
- A backup power system should be in place.
- Fuse box should be hidden and locked.

Safe Room

- Safe Room: The Safe Room is a strategically chosen room in the residence that would provide the best cover for the Principal in the event of a breach.
- The Safe Room must be easily accessible at anytime.
- The Safe Room must contain First Aid kits, food and water, communications and a fire exit where possible.

Principal's Office

- The Principal's office / most frequented room should be situated away from the main access point and above ground level. Consider proximity to Safe Room.
- The Principal's office should be fitted with curtains or blinds, armoured / strengthened windows and a panic alarm.
- The Principal's desk /chair should not be situated near windows.
- The PPO's room should be situated in close proximity to the Principal's office.

NOTES

6.4
Non-Security Staff Briefing

Non-Security Staff such as housekeepers and catering should be briefed the minimum of the following:

1. Keep all exterior doors closed and locked at all times including skylights and manholes.
2. Windows should be closed and locked during the day and all curtains / blinds drawn at night.
3. No visitors should be permitted access without the authority of the RST.
4. Do not accept or bring unauthorised / unchecked packages or envelopes into the residence.
5. No information is to be given to unknown individuals over the phone or anywhere else (either on-duty or off-duty).
6. Report anything out of the ordinary or suspicious to the RST, regardless how minor the detail appears to be (either on or off-duty).
7. If suspicious incidents involve individuals or vehicles, note description / plate number.
8. Do not touch suspicious items. Simply note the location and report to the RST immediately.
9. Sensitive documentation should be passed to the RST for disposal (burning).

NOTES

6.5
Handling Mail

Staff safety

- Designate selected trained staff to initially screen and open mail
- Wash your hands with hot water and soap before and after handling mail
- You may want to wear disposable medical-type gloves and particulate-or dust-type masks when working with mail
- Experts generally agree this may not be necessary on a continual basis
- Masks will decrease exposure but will not be 100% preventive
- Do not eat, drink or smoke around mail

Separate area

- Whenever possible, open mail in a single controlled area away from other employees.
- Open mail on a hard surface, such as a counter or table - not over a carpet.
- Select an area away from heating, air conditioning, ventilation systems and duct.
- Open mail and packages away from your body.
- Have various sizes of plastic bags, such as pint quart, gallon zip-lock, and garbage bags immediately available in work area

NOTES

Screening

Screen mail for the following characteristics. Any package or envelope that:

- Is unexpected or from someone unfamiliar to you
- Is addressed to someone no longer in your organization or otherwise outdated
- Does not have a return address, or the return address cannot be verified as legitimate
- Is of unusual weight, given its size, or is lopsided or oddly shaped
- Is marked with restricted endorsements, such as "personal" or "confidential"
- Has protruding wires, strange odors or stains
- Has a city or state in the postmark that does not match the return address or has no return address

NOTES

6.6
Suspicious Mail

Letter Bomb Recognition

- Foreign mail, air mail, and special delivery
- Restrictive markings, such as confidential, personal etc.
- Excessive or inadequate postage
- Handwritten or poorly typed address
- Incorrect titles
- Titles but no names
- Misspelling of common words
- Rub-on or block lettering
- Oily stains
- Visual distractions such as money or pornography
- Discolorations
- Smell
- No return address
- Excessive weight
- Contents are stiff
- Strange smell
- Lopsided or uneven envelope
- Protruding wires or tinfoil
- Excessive securing material, such as masking tape, string etc.

Control of Suspicious Mail

- Wear protective gloves / glasses.
- Seal mail in plastic bag.
- Evacuate and cordon the immediate area.
- Inform authorities.
- Place any contaminated clothes in plastic bag and seal.
- Wash hands and other areas of body that may have been contaminated.
- Quarantine anyone who came in contact with the item.
- List other affected persons (emergency services will require this).
- If item has spilled any substance, switch off ventilation systems.

Section 7
Surveillance Awareness

Surveillance is the systematic observation by covert or overt means of a person or location by visual, photographic or technical means.

Being surveillance aware will significantly reduce the likelihood of your Principal being targeted.

7.1
Who Conducts Surveillance?

- Terrorists
- Criminals
- Foreign intelligence agencies
- Press

Any plan requires gathering of information on the target in order to be effective. The aggressor gathers this information through surveillance over a period of time prior to a planned action or attack.

7.2
Aims Of Surveillance

- Identify the Security team
- Assess strength
- Identify weapons
- Identify vehicles and equipment
- Assess the Modus Operandi of the security team
- Identify capability and professionalism of security team
- Identify routine and pattern setting by the target
- TO GAIN AS MUCH INFO. AS POSSIBLE ON THE TARGET

REMEMBER – Off-duty does not mean switch off – you can be a target of surveillance at any time, not just with the Principal.

NOTES

7.3
Types Of Surveillance

- Foot
- Mobile (motor transport of any kind)
- Static (Observation Posts)
- Technical (Covert audio and video equipment etc.)
- Aerial (Helicopter etc.)

Surveillance Teams

- Level of training?
- Size / type of force?
- Types of Vehicle?
- Technical Equipment?

Each of these points will be directly relative to the size and resources of the organization ordering the surveillance.

Terrorist cells will likely have limited resources and as a result limited access to high tech equipment. This does not necessarily mean that the individuals conducting the surveillance will be any less capable.

High net worth Principals can often be the subject of governmental surveillance and as a result surveillance teams assigned to these tasks will likely have a broad spectrum of equipment and funding available to them.

Anti Surveillance

A system of drills employed by the team or a third party to deter, prevent or stop surveillance on the Principal or team.

Types Of Anti Surveillance

- Passive
- Covert
- Overt e.g. Decoy Principal, decoy vehicles.

NOTES

7.4
Counter Surveillance Planning

Counter Surveillance is the use of a third party to identify surveillance operations on the Principal or associated individuals, including the security team.

Examples of Counter Surveillance:

- Decoy Principal
- Decoy vehicles
- Empty moves
- Route Boxing (reciprocation of a planned but illogical route in order that an additional security team / vehicle identifies a criminal surveillance team)
- Cadence driving (an unnatural increase / decrease in speed, particularly effective on highways. Again, with the use of an additional team or vehicle).

NOTES

Intelligence

Intelligence is information that has been analyzed and refined so that it becomes useful to the owner.

Any information gained on the surveillance team should be processed as per the points below in order to extract the maximum intelligence on the hostile party.

Collate
(Collate information from all parties and individuals)

Analyze
(Analyze the information - every last detail)

Assess
(Assess the information to identify weaknesses or vulnerabilities in the hostile party)

Brief
(All information should be passed to every team member, an outline maybe briefed to the Principal if required)

Plan
(Decide what actions need to be taken to achieve your aim)

Act
(Execute the actions)

NOTES

Section 8
Armour

8.1
Ballistic Armour

Grading standards vary from country to country and between manufacturers. Two commonly used standards are the US National Institute of Justice (NIJ) and the UK Home Office Scientific Development Branch (HOSDB).

Choosing Armour

- Select the level of protection that suits the threat and conditions.
- Armour is a trade off between protection and comfort.
- Some types of armour is designed to withstand only one impact, not multiple strikes - check with the manufacturer.
- Replace body armour immediately if impacted or damaged to any extent.
- Hard armour is designed to be worn with accompanying soft body armour.
- Armour is weaker around the edges and therefore will not offer as much protection in the fringe areas.
- Not wearing soft with hard armour may reduce the protection of the latter. Check with the manufacturer which soft armour should accompany the hard armour.
- The higher the level of protection, the more cumbersome and restrictive it is to be worn.

The six main threat levels of ballistic armour

Level I Soft armour
Level IIA Soft armour
Level II Soft armour
Level IIIA Soft armour and some hard armour
Level III Hard (plated) armour
Level IV Hard (plated) armour

Hard Armour (Levels III and IV)

Levels III and IV are designed to defeat high velocity projectiles but must be used in conjunction with the soft body armour tested specifically for that combination.

Armour Specifications

NIJ Ratings

N.b. test calibres are subject to periodic revision by the testing organisations and as such details below may vary. Always check with the aforementioned bodies to confirm standards.

- **Level I**

The lowest level of ballistic protection.

Lvl I Test Calibres (5 strikes):	22 cal LR 40gr lead solid travelling between a speed of 1400fps and 1450fps.
	38 Special 158gr lead round nose travelling between a speed of 850 fps and 900fps.

- **Level IIA**

Level IIA offers protection against Level I threats and other lower threats as well as low and medium velocity .9mm and 357 magnum. Calibres such as the .45ACP and .32ACP etc are all lower threats.

Lvl IIA Test Calibres (5 strikes)	9mm 124gr full metal jacket (FMJ) travelling between a speed of 1090fps and 1140fps
	357 magnum 158gr jacketed soft point (JSP) travelling between a speed of 1250fps and 1300fps

- **Level II**

Level II offers protection against the same projectiles as Level IIA, but at higher velocities.

Lvl II Test Calibres (5 strikes)	9mm 124gr full metal jacket (FMJ) travelling between a speed of 1175fps and 1225fps
	357 magnum 158gr jacketed soft point (JSP) travelling between a speed of 1395fps and 1445fps

- **Level IIIA**

Normally the highest threat level in soft body armour.

Lvl IIIA Test Calibres (5 strikes)	9mm 124gr full metal jacket (FMJ) travelling between a speed of 1400fps and 1450fps which is sub machine gun velocity
	44 magnum 240gr lead semi wad cutter travelling between a speed of 1400fps and 1450fps

NOTES

- **Level III**

This threat level is a hard plate style of armour and is used in conjunction with soft body armour to give protection against high velocity projectiles. Some manufacturers produce plates that are stand-alone and can be used without soft body armour.

Lvl III Test Calibres (5 strikes):	7.62 x 51 FMJ (M80) travelling between a speed of 2750fps and 2800fps.

- **Level IV**

Hard plates: designed to defeat Armour Piercing (AP) projectiles and is tested with a single impact of the test calibre.

Lvl IV Test Calibre (1 strike):	30.06 M2AP 166gr (armour piercing) travelling between a speed of 2850fps and 2900fps.

European Standard DIN EN1063 Specifications

N.b. test calibres are subject to periodic revision by the testing organisations and as such details below may vary. Always check with the aforementioned bodies to confirm standards.

BR levels are also referred to as B levels. e.g. BR6 or B6 armoured vehicle.

Rating	Ammunition	Weight (grains)	Weight (grams)	min fps	max fps	Number of shots
BR1	.22 LR RN L	40	2.59	1048	1214	3
BR2	9 mm Luger FMJ-RN SC	124	8.04	1280	1345	3
BR3	.357 Magnum FMJ-CB SC	158	10.24	1378	1444	3
BR4	.44 Magnum FCJ-FN SC	240	15.55	1411	1476	3
BR5	5.56 mm x 45 NATO SS 109 steel penetrator	62	4.02	3084	3150	3
BR6	7.62 mm x 51 NATO M80 FMJ	147	9.53	2690	2756	3
BR7	7.62 mm x 51 NATO AP HC1	150	9.72	2657	2723	3
SG1/SG2, Shotgun	12 gauge solid lead slug	478	30.97	1312	1444	1

Ammunition Abbreviations

AP	Armour piercing
L	Lead
CB	Coned bullet
FMJ	Full metal jacket bullet
FN	Flat nose bullet
HC1	Steel hard core
PB	Hrc pointed bullet
RN	Round nose bullet
SC	Soft core (lead)
SCP1	Soft core (lead) with steel penetrator (type ss109)
SWC	Semi wad cutter
JSP	Jacket soft point

NOTES

Section 9
Crib cards

9.1
Contact Reports

Initial Contact Report

1. Callsign
2. Contact [type]
3. Wait Out

e.g. *"Echo 6, Contact Shooting, Wait out"*

Full Contact Report

A	Time (of Contact)
B	Location (as accurate as possible)
C	What Happened
D	What you did (reaction)
E	What you are doing now
F	What you require
G	Safe route (for any assisting callsigns / agencies)
H	Status of Principal (Unharmed / Walking Wounded / Critical)

NOTES

9.2
Casualty Reports

METHANE

M	Me (Your Callsign)
E	Exact Location
T	Type of Incident (e.g. IED)
H	Hazards in the area
A	Access Route (for responding callsigns)
N	Number of Casualties
E	Which emergency services / agencies required

NOTES

Nine Liner

Type of Info	Info	Remarks / Instructions	
Location of Pick Up Point	**Line 1** Grid / Spot Reference	Preferably full grid including prefix	
Frequency, Channel, Callsign	**Line 2** Comms details	Comms details of the person controlling casualties / area.	
Number of Casualties By Precedence	**Line 3** No. of casualties; Brevity code	A - Urgent B - Urgent surgical C - Priority D - Routine E - Convenience If two or more words must be reported in the same request, insert the proword BREAK between each category.	
Special Equipment Required	**Line 4** Brevity Code	A - None B - Hoist C - Extraction Equipment D - Ventilator	
Number of Casualties by Type	**Line 5** No. of Casualties; Brevity Code	L - Litter A - Ambulatory If both types are included in the same request, insert the proword BREAK between the types.	
Security of Pick Up Point	**Line 6** Brevity code.	N - No hostiles in the area P - Possible hostiles in area E - Hostiles in area, approach with caution X - Hostiles in area, armed escort required	
Methods of Marking Pick Up Point	**Line 7** Brevity code.	A - Panels B - Pyrotechnic signals C - Smoke signals D - None E - Other	
Casualty Nationality and Status	**Line 8** Brevity code. The number of casualties in each category is not transmitted	*PSD* **A** - Security Expat **B** - Client Expat **C** - Security Local National **D** - Client Local National **E** - Other	*US / UK mil* **A** - Military US / UK **B** - Civilian US / UK **C** - Military non-US / UK **D** - Civilian non-US / UK **E** - Hostile
CBRN Contamination	**Line 9** Brevity code	C - Chemical B - Biological R - Radioactive N - Nuclear	

9.3
Suspected Devices

A	What it is (Description of Object)
B	Where it is (exact location)
C	ICP location
D	Safe Route to ICP

NOTES

9.4
Incident Report

A	Incident Type (describe)
B	Name / Contact details of reporting person
C	Date of incident
D1	Location of incident
D2	Location description
E	Details of other staff involved
F	Details of third parties involved
G	Detailed description of incident
H	Details of any injuries sustained
I	Details of any local authorities involved. (Police, Medical, Fire, government agencies etc.)
J	Is the Principal / Client aware of the incident? (If not present at the occurrence)

NOTES

9.5
Bomb Threat Report

Conduct

- Write everything down.
- Ask questions.
- Keep the caller talking.
- Remain calm.
- Never threaten or insult the caller.
- Treat possible hoax as a real call until otherwise confirmed.

Information Requirements

When is the bomb going to explode?	
Where is it?	
What does it look like?	
What kind of bomb is it?	
What will initiate it?	
Who planted it?	
What is the caller's motivation?	
Where is the caller?	
What is the caller's name?	
What is the caller's address or area?	
Sex of caller?	
Phone number (Both receiving and originating):	
Estimated age:	
Description of caller's voice:	
Time call received	
Other:	

NOTES

9.6
Person / Vehicle Descriptions

Vehicle - SCRIM

Shape	
Colour	
Registration / Plate number	
Identifying features / marks	
Make / Model / year	

Person - A-HS

Age	
Build	
Clothing	
Distinguishing Features	
Elevation (height)	
Face	
Gait	
Hair	
Sex	

NOTES

Section 10
Useful Open Source Links

News

World News Search http://wn.com/sitemap
Global Incident Map http://www.globalincidentmap.com/map.php

Mapping

Afghanistan Maps http://www.lib.utexas.edu/maps/afghanistan.html
Africa Maps http://www.lib.utexas.edu/maps/africa/
Global Incident Map http://www.globalincidentmap.com/map.php

Flight Travel

Airport Database http://www.world-airport-database.com
Airport Codes http://www.world-airport-codes.com

Embassies

World Embassies Database http://www.embassyworld.com

Health

Map of Disease Outbreaks around the world http://www.healthmap.org/en/

Weather

Real-time Weather Database http://weather.noaa.gov

NOTES

Section 11
Abbreviations

11.1
General Abbreviations

A&E	Accident and Emergency department
AAR	After Action Review
Atts	Attachments
C2	Command and Control
C3	Command, Control and Communications
CBRN	Chemical, Biological, Radioactive, Nuclear
CEI	Communication Electronic Instructions
Comms	Communications
CP	Close Protection
Dets	Detachments
EP	Executive Protection
Eqpt	Equipment
FPS	Feet per second
GPS	Global Positioning System
GSM	Global System for Mobile Communications
Helo	Helicopter
HF	High Frequency
HOSDB	Home Office Scientific Development Branch
ICP	Incident Control Point
IED	Improvised Explosive Device
LHT	Left Hand Traffic
MDCOA	Most Dangerous Course of Action
MLCOA	Most Likely Course of Action
NIJ	National Institute for Justice
OST	Office Security Team
PES	Personal Escort Section
POC	Point of Contact
PPO	Personal Protection Officer
PSD	Protective Security Detail

RFI	Request for Information
RHT	Right Hand Traffic
RST	Residential Security team
RTA	Road Traffic Accident
Satnav	Satellite Navigation system
TAM	Tactical Aide Memoire
Taskorg	Task Organisation
UHF	Ultra High Frequency
UNI	Unique Numerical Identifier
VHF	Very High Frequency

NOTES

11.2
Iraq Abbreviations

APT	Armed Protection Team
AQI	Al-Qaeda
AQIZAM	Al-Qaeda in Iraq and Associated Movements
BIAP	Baghdad International Airport
BOLO	Be On Look Out
CLC	Concerned Local Citizens
COB	Contingency Operating Base
CP	Checkpoint
CQA	Close Quarters Assassination
DBS	Drive By Shooting
DoD	US Department of Defence
EFP	Explosively Formed Projectile
EOD	Explosive Ordinance Disposal
ERW	Explosive Remnants of War
FOB	Forward Operating Base
FoM	Freedom of Movement
FP	Federal Police
GoI	Government of Iraq
HG	Hand Grenade
HME	Home Made Explosive
IA	Iraqi Army
IDF	Indirect Fire
IED	Improvised Explosive Device
IHEC	Iraqi High Electoral Commission
IP	Iraqi Police
IPS	Iraqi Police Service
IRL	Improvised Rocket Launcher
ISF	Iraqi Security Forces
ISI	Islamic State of Iraq
IZ	International Zone (Green Zone)
JSS	Joint Security Station
MAIED	Magnetic IED

PM	Prime Minister
POI	Point Of Impact
POO	Point Of Origin
PPO	Personal Protection Officer
PSC	Private Security Company
PSD	Private Security Detail
RPG	Rocket Propelled Grenade
SAF	Small Arms Fire
SAFIRE	Surface to Air Fire
SEG	Sunni Extremist Group
SIIC	Supreme Iraq Islamic Council
SoI	Sons of Iraq
SVBIED	Suicide Vehicle Borne IED
SVEST	Suicide Vest Bomber
SVIED	Suicide Vest IED
TTP	Tactics, Techniques and Procedures
USF-I	US Forces Iraq
UVIED	Under Vehicle IED
VBIED	Vehicle Borne IED
VCP	Vehicle Check Point

NOTES

11.3
Afghanistan Abbreviations

AA&E	Ammunition AND Explosives
ABP	Afghanistan Border Police
ACD	Afghanistan Customs Department
ACF	Anti-Coalition Forces
ACGHO	Afghanistan Cartography and Geodesy Head Office
AEP	Afghan Expatriate Program
AGE	Anti-Government Elements / Extremists
AGO	Attorney General's Office
AIHRC	Afghan Independent Human Rights Commission
AIMS	Afghanistan Information Management System
aka	Also Known As
AMF	Afghan Militia Forces
ANA	Afghanistan National Army
ANAP	Afghanistan National Auxiliary Police
ANBP	Afghanistan New Beginning Program
ANCOP	Afghan National Civil Order Police
ANDS	Afghanistan National Development Strategy
ANP	Afghanistan National Police
ANSF	Afghan National Security Forces
ANSO	Afghanistan NGO Security Office
ARC	Afghanistan Red Crescent
ASR	Alternate Supply Route
AP	Anti Personnel
ASF	AFGHAN Special Forces
AT	Anti Tank
BAF	Bagram Air Field
BBIED	Body Borne Improvised Explosive Device
BDA	Battle Damage Assessment
BFT	Blue Force Tracker
BLO	Border Liaison Officer
BME	Bomb Making Equipment
BOLO	Be On the Lookout

C2	Command and Control
CAA	Civil Aviation Authority
CAS	Close Air Support
CF	Coalition Forces
CI	Counter Intelligence
CIT	Cash in Transit
CJTF	Combined Joint Task Force
CNJTF	Counter-Narcotics Justice Task Force
CN	Counter-Narcotics
CNPA	Counter-Narcotics Prosecution Agency
CNTF	Counter-Narcotics Trust Fund
CN	Counter Narcotics
CNTU	Counter-Narcotics Training Unit
COA	Course of Action
COIN OPS	Counter Insurgency Operations
CoP	Chief of Police
CP	Check Point
CPX	Complex attack
CQA	Close Quarter Assassination
DAB	Da Afghanistan Bank
DAC	District Administrative Centre
DC	District Centre
DDR	Disarmament, Demobilization & Reintegration
DF	Direct Fire
DIAG	Disbandment of Illegal Armed Groups
DRSG	Deputy Representative of the Secretary General
DoRR	Department of Refugees and Repatriation
EC	European Commission
ECM	Electronic Counter Measures
EFP	Explosively Formed Projectile
FNU	First Name Unknown
EDD	Explosive Detection Dog
EOD	Explosive Ordnance Disposal
EOF	Escalation of Force

FOB	Forward Operating Base
FP	Firing Point
FW	Fixed Wing
GIAAC	General Administration of Anti- Corruption
GoA	Government of Afghanistan
GR	Grid Reference (Provided in MGRS)
HCN	Host Country National
HF	Health Facility
HIG	Hizb-i-Islami Gulbuddin
HIK	Hizb-i-Islami Khalis
HMG	Heavy Machine Gun
HQ	Headquarters
HQN	Haqqani Network
HUMINT	Human Intelligence
HVT	High Value Target
IA	Intelligence Analyst
IAG	Illegally armed group
ICC	International Criminal Court
IDF	Indirect fire (Rockets and mortars)
IDLG	Independent Directorate of Local Governance
IDP	Internally Displaced Person
IED	Improvised Explosive Device
IMF	International Military Forces
IMINT	Imagery Intelligence
IMU	Islamic Movement of Uzbekistan
INS	Insurgents
IOT	In order to
IRAM	Improvised Rocket Assisted Mortar
IRC	International Red Cross
IRoA	Islamic Republic of Afghanistan
ISAF	International Security Assistance Force
ISI	Pakistan Inter-Service Intelligence
IVO	In the Vicinity Of
JEMB	Joint Election Management Body

KAF	Kandahar Airfield
KAIA	Kabul International Airport
KCP	Kabul City Police
KIA	Killed in action
LEL	Lashkar-e-Islami
LN	Local National
MCN	Ministry of Counter Narcotics
MI	Military Intelligence
MIA	Missing in Action
MO	Modus Operandi
MoA&I	Ministry of Agriculture & Irrigation
MoC	Ministry of Communications
MoCI	Ministry of Commerce & Industry
MoCN	Ministry of Counter-Narcotics
MoCY	Ministry of Culture & Youth
MoD	Ministry of Defence
MoE	Ministry of Education
MoEW	Ministry of Energy & Water
MoF	Ministry of Finance
MoFA	Ministry of Foreign Affairs
MoHE	Ministry of Higher Education
MoI	Ministry of Interior
MoJ	Ministry of Justice
MoLSMD	Ministry of Labour, Social Affairs, Martyrs and Disabled
MoM	Ministry of Mines
MoPH	Ministry of Public Health
MoPW	Ministry of Public Works
MoRR	Ministry of Refugees & Repatriation
MoTCA	Ministry of Transport & Civil Aviation
MoUD	Ministry of Urban Development
MoWA	Ministry of Women's Affairs
MP	Military Police
MRRD	Ministry of Rural Rehabilitation and Development
MSR	Main Supply Route

NATO	North Atlantic Treaty Organisation
NDS	National Security Directorate
NFDK	No Further Detail Known
NGO	Non-Governmental Organisation
NFI	No further information
NPCC	National Police Command Centre
NSTR	Nothing Significant to Report
OAG	Office of the Attorney General
OEF	Operation Enduring Freedom
OGA	Other Government Agency
OP	Observation Point
PB	Patrol base
PD	Police District
PEF	Poppy Eradication Force
POA	President of Afghanistan
POC	Point of Contact
POI	Point of Impact
POO	Point of Origin
PPIED	Pressure Plate IED
PRT	Provincial Reconstruction Team
PSC	Private Security Company
PSD	Protective Security Detail
QRF	Quick Reaction Force
RCIED	Remote Control IED
ROE	Rules of Engagement
RPG	Rocket Propelled Grenade
RRN	Ring Road Network
RTA	Road Traffic Accident
RW	Rotary Wing
SAF	Small Arms Fire
SAFIRE	Surface to Air Fire
SAM	Surface to Air Missile
SBF	Support by Fire
SD	Surveillance Detection

SF	Security Forces
SOF	Special Operations Forces
Shura	Afghan local council of elders
SIGINT	Signal Intelligence
SOP	Standard Operating Procedures
SVBIED	Suicide VBIED
TB	Taliban
TBD	To be Determined
TCN	Third Country National
TCP	Traffic Control Point
TIC	Troops in contact
TOC	Tactical Operations Centre
TOO	Target of Opportunity
TTP	Tactics, Techniques and Procedures
UAV	Unmanned Aerial Vehicle
UGV	Upper Gereshk Valley (Helmand Province)
UGL	Under-Barrel Grenade Launcher (rifle-mounted grenade launcher)
UN	United Nations
UNAMA	United Nations Assistance Mission in Afghanistan
UNCAC	United Nations Convention Against Corruption
UNCHS	United Nations Centre for Human Settlements (Habitat)
UNDP	United Nations Development Program
UNDSS	United Nations Department of Safety and Security
UNESCO	United Nations Educational, Scientific and Cultural Organization
UNEP	United Nations Environment Program
UNFAO	United Nations Food and Agricultural Organization
UNICE	United Nations Children's Fund
UNIMF	International Monetary Fund
UNMACA	United Nation Mine Action Centre for Afghanistan
UNODC	United Nations Office for Drug Control
UNSRSG	Special Representative of the UN Secretary General
UN WFC	World Food Council
UN WFP	World Food Program
UN	World Health Organization

UNHCR	United Nations High Commission for Refugees
USAID	United States Agency for International Development
USE	United States Embassy
USV	Upper Sangin Valley (Helmand Province)
UXO	Unexploded Ordinance
VBIED	Vehicle Borne Improvised Explosive Device
VCP	Vehicle Check Point (Also, IVCP – Illegal VCP)
WB	World Bank
WIA	Wounded in action
WFP	World Food Programme
WHO	World Health Organisation

18780251R00089